Frans Hals: Style and Substance

WALTER LIEDTKE

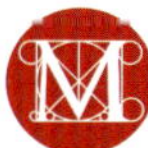

THE METROPOLITAN MUSEUM OF ART, NEW YORK

DISTRIBUTED BY YALE UNIVERSITY PRESS, NEW HAVEN AND LONDON

Reprint of *The Metropolitan Museum of Art Bulletin* (Summer 2011)

This publication is made possible through the generosity of the Lila Acheson Wallace Fund for The Metropolitan Museum of Art, established by the cofounder of *Reader's Digest*.

This publication is issued in conjunction with the exhibition "Frans Hals in the Metropolitan Museum," on view at The Metropolitan Museum of Art, New York, from July 26 to October 10, 2011.

The exhibition is generously made possible by Bernard and Louise Palitz.

Published by The Metropolitan Museum of Art, New York
Publisher and Editor in Chief: Mark Polizzotti
Associate Publisher and General Manager: Gwen Roginsky
Editor of the *Bulletin*: Sue Potter
Production Manager: Christopher Zichello
Designer: Katy Homans

Front cover: Frans Hals, *Young Man and Woman in an Inn* (*"Yonker Ramp and His Sweetheart"*), 1623 (detail; see fig. 18, page 20). Back cover: Frans Hals, *Paulus Verschuur*, 1643 (detail; see fig. 31, page 31). Inside front and back covers: Frans Hals, *Petrus Scriverius* and *Anna van der Aar*, 1626 (both enlarged; see figs. 37, 38, pages 38–39)

Cataloging-in-Publication data is available from the Library of Congress.
ISBN: 978-1-58839-424-8 (The Metropolitan Museum of Art)
ISBN: 978-0-300-16982-9 (Yale University Press)

Printed and bound in the United States of America.

The Metropolitan Museum of Art
1000 Fifth Avenue
New York, NY 10028
metmuseum.org

Distributed by
Yale University Press, New Haven and London
yalebooks.com/art
yalebooks.co.uk

The author would like to extend special thanks to Christopher Atkins, Seymour Slive, and Dennis Weller.

DIRECTOR'S NOTE

The Metropolitan Museum has the largest and most representative ensemble of paintings by the great Dutch master Frans Hals (1582/83–1666) to be found outside his hometown of Haarlem in the Netherlands. The collection contains eleven autograph works—seven portraits and four genre scenes—plus a portrait and a genre picture once thought to be by Hals.

In a broader view, the number of paintings by Hals in New York public collections—there are four portraits in the Frick Collection and one in the Brooklyn Museum—might be expected in a city and country where for two hundred years Dutch pictures have been preferred to those of other European schools, and where portraits of distinctive individuals (whether by Hals, Rembrandt, Van Dyck, or less famous masters) were long preferred to other figure paintings.

But there is more to the story than that. Until recently the staircase leading up to the main floor of the Rijksmuseum in Amsterdam had a large sign hanging overhead: "Hals – Rembrandt – Vermeer." This did not mean that some fifty-five rooms of Medieval, Renaissance, and later paintings, sculpture, and decorative arts had been roped off or that the collection lacked works by hundreds of other Dutch painters. The sign simply served as a beacon to local and foreign visitors who since about 1900 had considered those three artists to be the giants of the Golden Age.

At any time between about 1670 and 1870 neither Hals nor Vermeer would have been cited in the same breath as Rembrandt. Vermeer was little known beyond the vicinity of his native Delft during his lifetime, and his small oeuvre was only beginning to be "rediscovered" from the 1860s onward. Hals, by contrast, has been familiar to critics and collectors since his own time, but for nearly two hundred years he fell out of favor because the academic priorities of drawing, fine finish, and elevated subject matter were lacking in his work.

With the Realist movement in France and elsewhere in the second half of the nineteenth century, Hals's "democratic" subjects and seemingly impressionistic style made him an inspiration to artists such as Gustave Courbet, Édouard Manet, Claude Monet, Vincent van Gogh, John Singer Sargent, James McNeill Whistler, William Merritt Chase, and many others. Haarlem became a mecca for modern painters after its Municipal Museum opened in 1862, and Hals became one of the old masters who should be represented in any important collection. And indeed that is how the Met came to hold such a strong representation of the artist. Legendary American collectors such as Henry Marquand, Jules Bache, Benjamin Altman, and Mrs. H. O. Havemeyer all acquired works by Hals and eventually gave them to the Met, the earliest arriving in 1889 and the last in 1949.

In this *Bulletin* Walter Liedtke, who for thirty years has been the Museum's curator of Dutch and Flemish paintings, contributes an original essay on Hals's style and its expressive purpose. The publication complements the fifty pages on Hals in his collection catalogue *Dutch Paintings in The Metropolitan Museum of Art* and a *Bulletin* by Esmée Quodbach on the formation of that collection, both published in 2007. This *Bulletin* accompanies the exhibition "Frans Hals in the Metropolitan Museum," which opens on July 26 and continues through October 10, 2011, and which includes not only our own paintings by the master but also two great Halses from private collections and eleven pictures by artists who set his work in context. The Museum is grateful to the lenders to the exhibition and to Bernard and Louise Palitz for funding this important show.

Thomas P. Campbell
Director, The Metropolitan Museum of Art

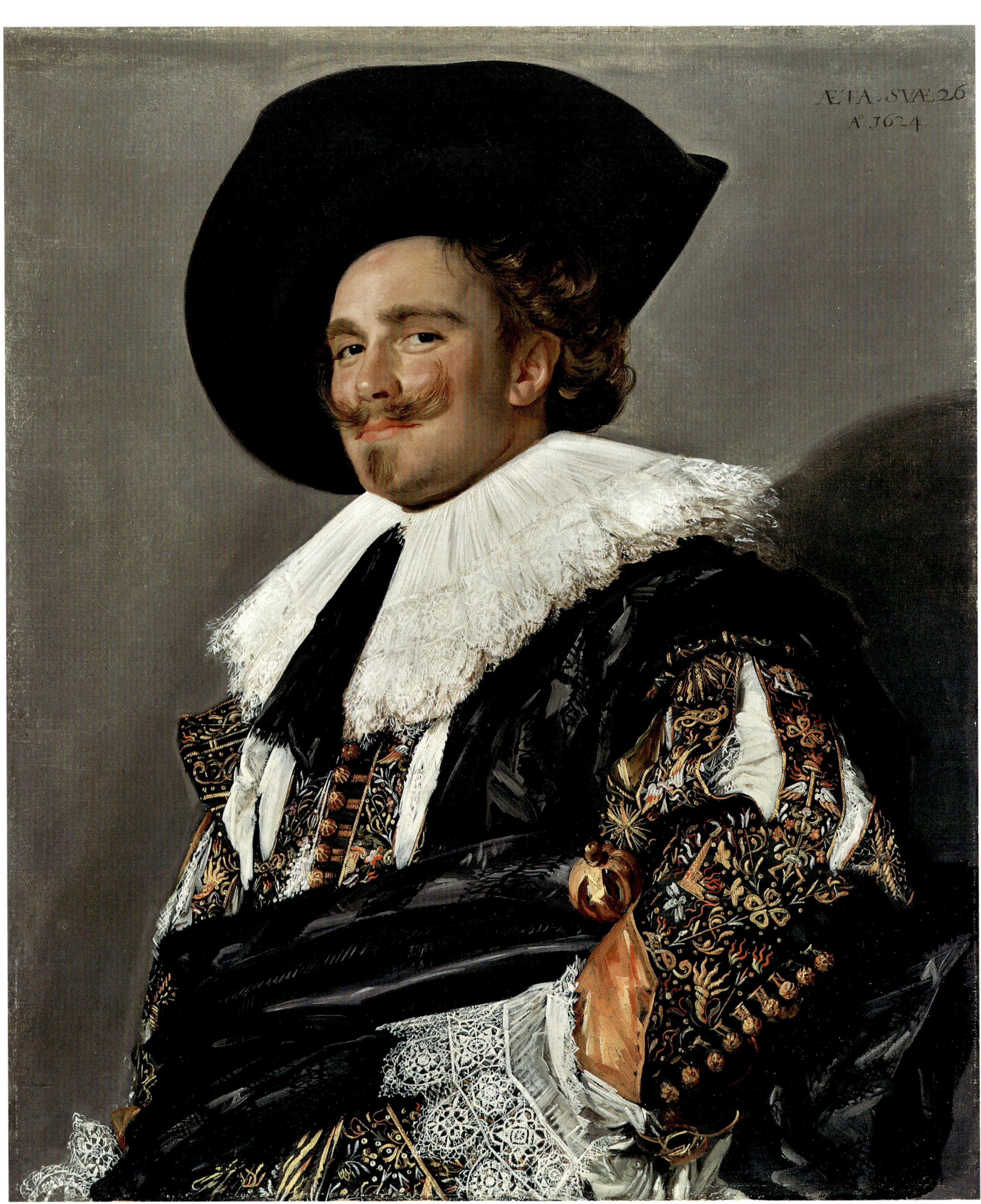
ÆTA . SVÆ 26
A° 1624

Frans Hals: Style and Substance

The name of Frans Hals (1582/83–1666) instantly evokes images of bourgeois bonhomie, and has done so since the middle of the nineteenth century. Admirers will readily recognize such widely reproduced works as *The Laughing Cavalier* (fig. 1), *Young Man and Woman in an Inn* (fig. 18), and at least one or two of the great group portraits of Haarlem civic guard companies (see figs. 8, 16), which all remain in Haarlem and still look (as they must have when they were first displayed) like tableaux vivants of the banquets that, according to a municipal ordinance, were not supposed to last more than three or four days. This convivial notion of Hals (in both his first and last names the *a* is flat, as in "ah," and the *s* is sibilant, like the "ce" in "flounce") has been advanced by writers from Henry James, in his 1872 essay on the Metropolitan's inaugural exhibition, to the modern doyen of Hals scholarship, Seymour Slive. The idea of Hals as sympathetically amused by his fellow man has been taken rather far, however, especially with regard to some of his male portraits. For example, the sitter generally known since 1888 as "the Laughing Cavalier" (fig. 1) is neither of those things, but a wealthy and fashionable gentleman whose restrained smile is as much an assumed form of self-presentation as the emblematic embroidery on his jacket, the gilded hilt of his sword (implying a person of considerable privilege), and the position of his near arm, a pose recently dubbed "the Renaissance elbow" (as seen in Bronzino's portrait of a slightly smiling aristocrat from the 1530s; fig. 2).[1]

Today more than half of Hals's sitters are unidentified, but in the nineteenth century the number was much higher and was complemented by mistaken identifications or simple indifference to the historical significance of reliable names. Thus the still anonymous "cavalier" and the wealthy textile merchant, collector, and philanthropist Willem van Heythuysen (fig. 3) could have been seen as suitable models for the swashbuckling heroes in *The Three Musketeers*, Alexandre Dumas's novel of 1844 (see fig. 4). But to read Hals's characterizations in these terms would be off the mark: Van Heythuysen never even joined one of Haarlem's civic guard companies (as one would expect of such a prominent citizen), to say nothing of racing around France with his rapier drawn.

A similar case is found in the lines the German cataloguer Gustav Waagen devoted

1. Frans Hals (Dutch, Antwerp 1582/83–1666 Haarlem). *The Laughing Cavalier*, 1624. Oil on canvas, 33⅞ x 27⅛ in. (86 x 69 cm). The Wallace Collection, London (P84). The title was invented in England between 1875 and 1888. The twenty-six-year-old (according to the inscription in the upper right corner) sitter, almost certainly a bachelor, wears a highly stylish jacket embroidered with symbols referring to love: arrows, bees, flames, lovers' knots, and so on. The costume and sword (with its gilded pommel) suggest a rich and cultivated gentleman rather than a "cavalier" or any kind of military man.

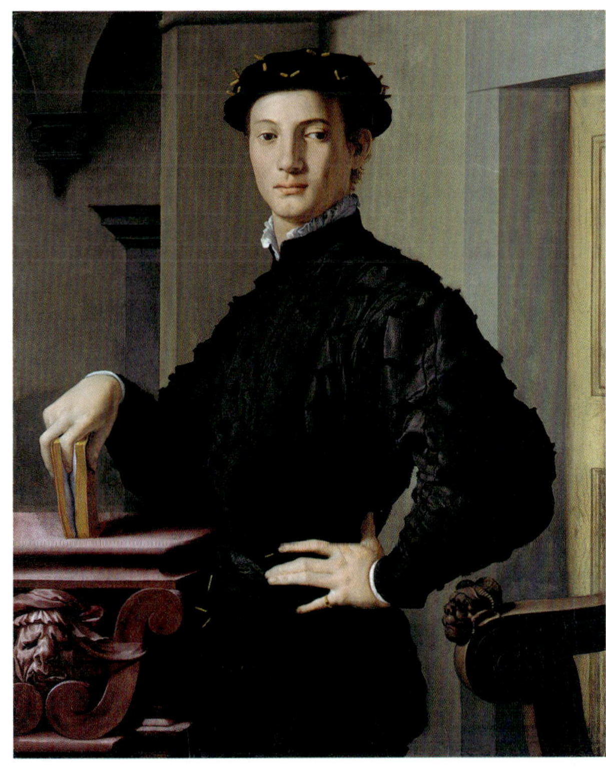

2. Bronzino (Italian, Monticelli 1503–1572 Florence). *Portrait of a Young Man*, 1530s. Oil on wood, 37⅝ x 29½ in. (95.6 x 74.9 cm). The Metropolitan Museum of Art, H. O. Havemeyer Collection, Bequest of Mrs. H. O. Havemeyer, 1929 (29.100.16)

3. Frans Hals. *Willem van Heythuysen*, ca. 1625. Oil on canvas, 80½ x 53 in. (204.5 x 134.5 cm). Alte Pinakothek, Bayerische Staatsgemäldesammlungen, Munich (14101). Large full-length portraits were exceptional in the northern Netherlands, and this is Hals's only known example. The princely format, probably derived from English court portraits, appears to have been introduced about 1618 by the Amsterdam artist Cornelis van der Voort (1576–1624). The magnificent sword and the setting (an imaginary country estate) amplify the impression that Van Heythuysen aspired to the stature of nobility.

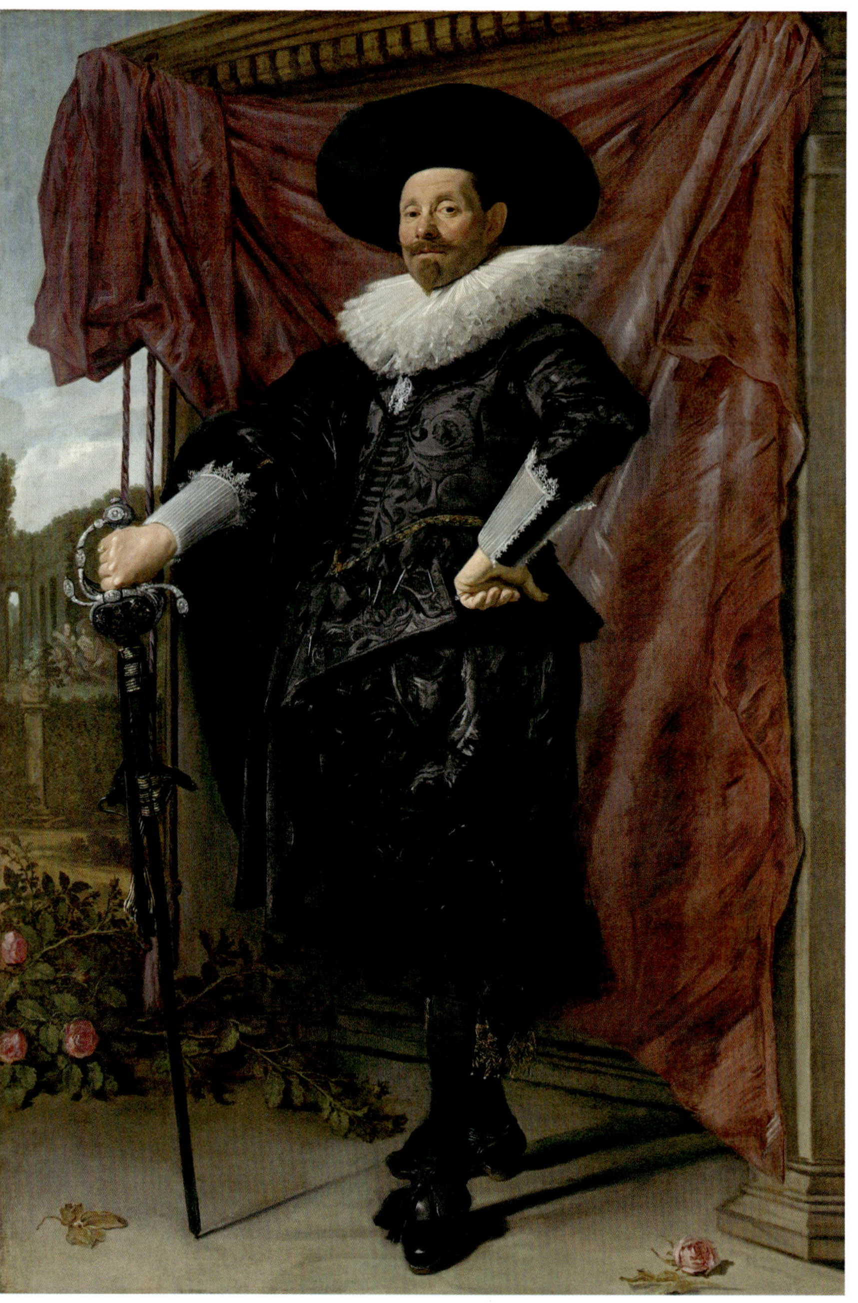

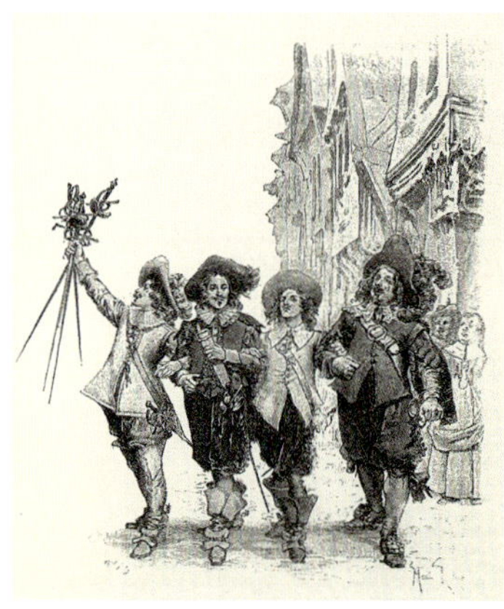

4. Maurice Leloir (French, 1853–1940). "They walked Arm-in-Arm, occupying the whole Width of the Street." From Alexandre Dumas, *The Three Musketeers* (New York and Boston, 1894), vol. 1, p. 61. Leloir was a Parisian painter, engraver, playwright, and prolific illustrator. His illustrations to the 1894 edition of *Les trois mousquetaires* led to his work in 1928–29 on Douglas Fairbanks's film *The Man in the Iron Mask*, a sequel to his *The Three Musketeers* of 1921. Leloir was also a scholar of historical costume, drawing extensively on paintings and prints of the relevant periods.

5. Frans Hals. *Portrait of a Man, possibly Nicolaes Pietersz Duyst van Voorhout*, ca. 1636–38. Oil on canvas, 31¾ x 26 in. (80.6 x 66 cm). The Metropolitan Museum of Art, The Jules Bache Collection, 1949 (49.7.33). Duyst van Voorhout, who evidently never married, was a wealthy brewer and collector in Haarlem. His satin jacket is especially stylish.

to Hals's *Portrait of a Man, possibly Nicolaes Pietersz Duyst van Voorhout* (fig. 5) in 1854. The "cavalier" pose is here repeated and the costume is again swank. In Waagen's analysis the fleshy figure's eyes and cheeks betray "many a sacrifice to Bacchus," as if the man—like Hals himself, according to Arnold Houbraken's inventive biography of 1718—could usually be found in a tavern rather than working at home. A hundred and twenty years later, Slive maintained that Waagen's "estimate of the model's drinking habits was virtually substantiated when it was discovered that the man portrayed was Claes Duyst van Voorhout, owner of [a brewery]."[2] Leaving aside the evidence for the sitter's identity, which is uncertain, and the question of whether brewers drank a large part of what they produced, it should be taken into account that the owners of breweries in Haarlem, Delft, and other Dutch cities were usually highly regarded citizens, a number of whom held important government offices

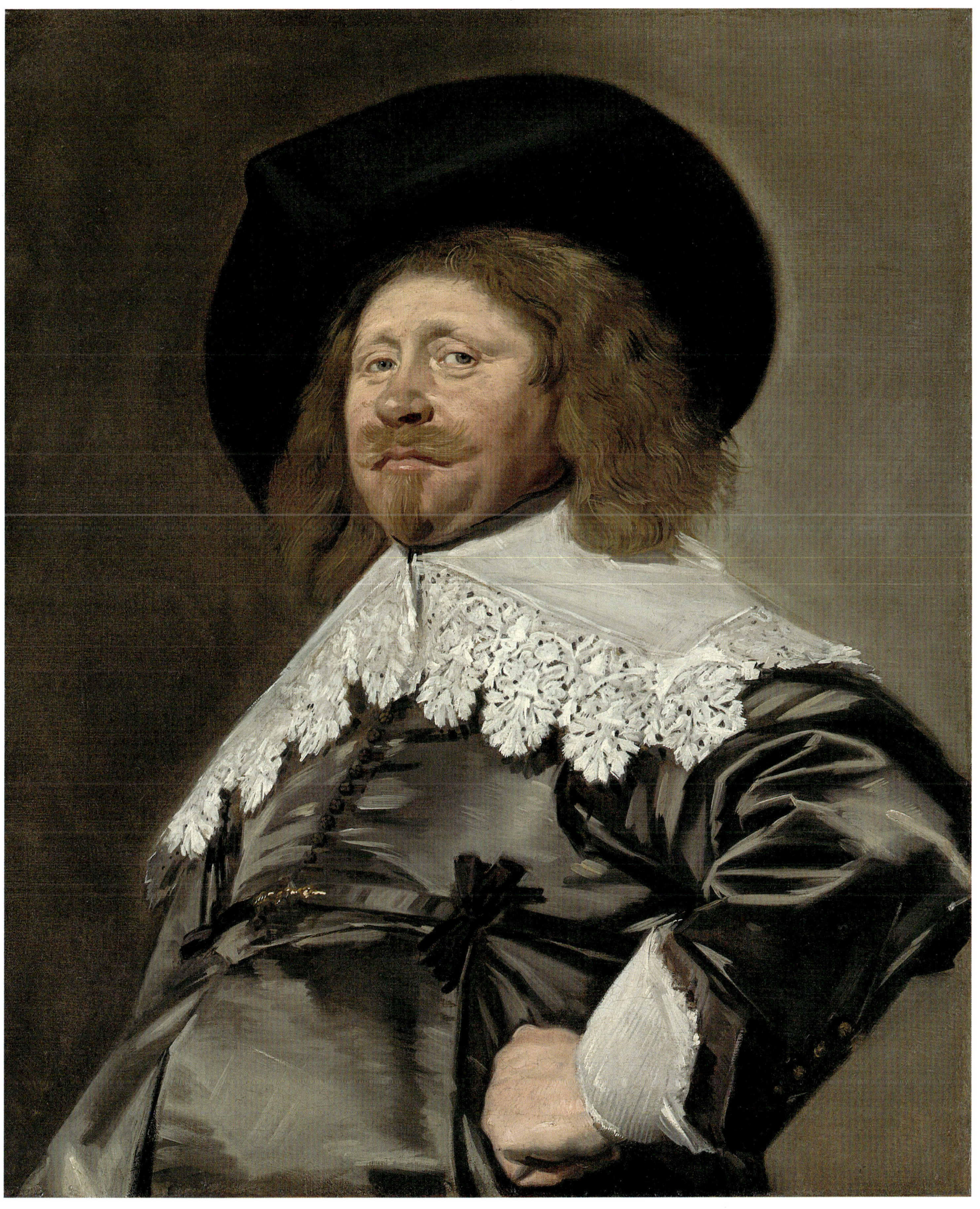

(which at least in that culture was a sign of respectability and social position). Beer was the staple beverage of the period, low in alcoholic content and, unlike water, safe to drink. Rivaled only by textile manufacturing as a source of wealth in the Dutch Republic, brewing was the profession of leading families in Haarlem before and during Hals's career. After a political shakeup in 1618 (which ousted Catholics and other troublesome types), twenty-one of the twenty-four members of the Haarlem city council were brewers. As Pieter Biesboer, the recently retired curator of the Frans Hals Museum in Haarlem, expressed it, "this coterie of new regents became the core of Hals's clientele."[3]

The sitter in the Museum's brilliantly painted portrait, with his sober and perhaps even melancholic expression (another fashion of the time), was most likely such a person, and of course he had something to say about how Hals depicted him. We know very little about Nicolaes (or Claes) Pietersz Duyst van Voorhout (ca. 1600–1650) other than that he owned a brewery called The Swan's Neck in 1629, that his father, Pieter Claes Duyst van Voorhout, had been a brewer, and that when Nicolaes died he possessed forty-seven paintings, including works ascribed to Rubens, Hendrick Goltzius, and various well-known marine and still-life painters. (As was often the case with portraits listed in estate inventories of the period, none of the nine in Duyst van Voorhout's collection was attributed to a particular artist.) This suggests that the person portrayed by Hals was a gentleman of means and taste rather than a diurnal drunk. Such an illogical inference (are the heirs to vineyards all winos?) must have been encouraged not only by hazy notions of Haarlem society but also by Hals's posthumous reputation for bad behavior. Slive himself has done much to set the record straight but concedes that "popular notions regarding the master's disreputable conduct" have not changed: "the fallacious idea that an artist who depicted merry drinkers [as in all four of the Museum's genre scenes by Hals: figs. 14, 18, 24, 42] must needs have been a tosspot himself dies hard."[4]

Fictionalized accounts of famous artists were a flourishing subgenre of literature in the nineteenth century. Elbert Hubbard's *Little Journeys to the Homes of Eminent Painters* (1899), recounts, for example, that Rubens—the sort of Continental aesthete that most Americans considered suspect—taught members of the Spanish court how to roll cigarettes while engaged in conversation. Hals's reputation for drinking goes back to a much earlier source, Houbraken's colorful account of 1718. The Dordrecht author and history painter retells the familiar tale from Pliny's *Natural History* (35.81–83) of the painter Apelles paying an anonymous visit to the distant studio of Protogenes, and then "recalls" a similar story about Anthony van Dyck and Hals: While on his way to the court of Charles I (stand-in for Apelles's patron, Alexander the Great), Van Dyck made a detour to Haarlem just to meet Hals. The master was not at home and "it took some time to scour the taverns for him." Once found, Hals quickly tossed off a portrait of the unknown visitor, who then asked if he might try his hand ("Is this, then, how one paints?"). As soon as Hals saw the portrait of himself he exclaimed, "You are Van Dyck, for none but he could do this." (Protogenes had likewise identified Apelles from the fine line he had left on a panel as his calling card.) Several well-worn themes are at work here: virtuosity in a modern manner (Hals seen as Van Dyck's counterpart in brilliant brushwork), Dutch artists' parity with major artists from foreign lands, and flawed character as a roadblock to a great career. "Van Dyck went to great lengths to entice him to England, but [Hals] would not listen, being too attached to his dissolute ways." After praising "the boldness and vivacity with which [Hals's] brush

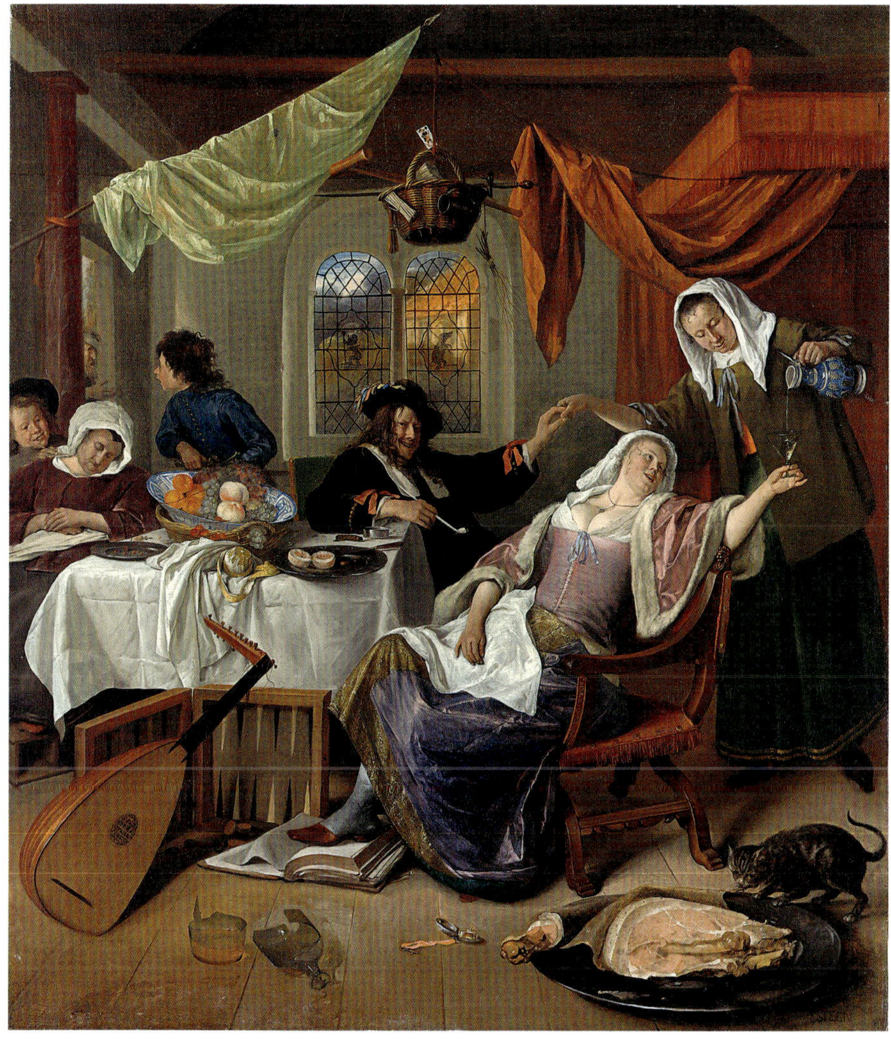

6. Jan Steen (Dutch, Leiden 1626–1679 Leiden). *The Dissolute Household*, 1660s. Oil on canvas, 42 ½ x 35 ½ in. (108 x 90.2 cm). The Metropolitan Museum of Art, The Jack and Belle Linsky Collection, 1982 (1982.60.31). Steen and his family lived in Haarlem during the 1660s, when he painted this and similar pictures of everyday life run amok. The seated couple strongly resemble the artist and his wife, Margriet van Goyen. The maid and master of the house join hands in the vulgar gesture that Hals assigned to the habitually improper Hans Worst in *Merrymakers at Shrovetide* (fig. 14).

caught the natural likeness" of his sitters, Houbraken cautions that this manner of execution is what apprentice painters should take as their model, "not his manner of living," for he often "gave his passions free rein."[5]

Houbraken's judgment was clearly deduced from Hals's genre pictures, quite as his biographies of Adriaen Brouwer, Jan Steen, Frans van Mieris, and other painters bring to mind their scenes set in taverns, bordellos, or "Jan Steen households." In his several pages on Steen, Houbraken states at the outset that his "comic life would fill a whole book," and that "his paintings are like his way of life and his way of life like his paintings." Today the quite respectable if not always smooth circumstances of Steen's life are well known. His father was a prosperous brewer in Leiden and his mother the daughter of the city clerk. There is no contemporary account of a drunken or disorderly lifestyle and plenty of evidence that Steen was a respected citizen and guild member in Leiden, The Hague, and Haarlem. Nonetheless, the fact that the artist helped his father run a brewery in Delft during the mid-1650s, along with paintings in which Steen and his wife play cameo roles (as in fig. 6), was enough evidence for Houbraken to report that in Delft Jan "returned to his old ways, buying wine [for himself] with his money instead of malt [for the customers]."[6]

Several other stories of this kind (his melodramatic biography of the painter Emanuel de Witte is a striking example) indicate that Houbraken's influential remarks about Hals cannot be trusted. Like his teacher Samuel van Hoogstraten

(1627–1678), Houbraken introduced the names of ancient and well-known modern masters not for the sake of art history but as art "theory" (criticism), which at the time was loaded with notions of polite learning, elevated subject matter, social stature, and prestigious patronage. Houbraken, himself a painter of biblical and mythological scenes, was almost prepared to write his lives of Hals and Steen simply by knowing what type of pictures they painted: in his view, low-life themes were treated by lowbrow artists. This sort of snobbery lasted far into the nineteenth century. The great English art critic John Ruskin launched numerous tirades against the typical subjects and styles of "the various Van somethings and Back somethings," a prejudice he absorbed early on from his teacher the watercolorist John Duffield Harding, according to Ruskin "a violent hater of the old Dutch school, and I imagine the first who told me that they were 'sots, gamblers, debauchees, delighting in the reality of the alehouse more than in its pictures.'"[7] Similarly, more than a century later Somerset Maugham famously told his lover Alan Searle when they were reunited after having been apart for much of the war: "You may have looked like a Bronzino once, but now you look like a depraved Frans Hals."[8]

When Steen moved to Haarlem in 1660, Hals was about seventy-eight years old and still had six years of work and two important commissions ahead of him (see fig. 41). He was born in Antwerp in 1582 or 1583, the son of Franchoys Hals (ca. 1542–before May 1610), a clothworker from Mechelen (Malines). The nominally Catholic family evidently left Flanders for the northern Netherlands by 1586. Frans's brother Dirck, who went on to paint "Merry Companies" (see fig. 20), was baptized in Haarlem in March 1591, as a Protestant. This suggests that the family, like many others, fled the Spanish Netherlands for religious as well as economic reasons.

The earliest document of Frans Hals himself records his entry in 1610 as a master in the Haarlem painters' guild.[9] At the time he was already twenty-seven or twenty-eight years old, an unusually advanced age at which to enter a guild for the first time. According to the anonymous biography of Karel van Mander (1548–1606) in the posthumous second edition of that Haarlem master's *Schilder-Boeck* (Painter Book) published in 1618, "Frans Hals, portrait painter of Haarlem" was one of Van Mander's many pupils. If so, this would have been before Van Mander left Haarlem in 1603 (which is plausible: most Dutch painters were on their own by about the age of twenty). It was also in 1610 or early in 1611 that Hals married twenty-year-old Anneke Harmensdr. Their son, the painter Harmen Hals (1611–1669), was baptized on September 2, 1611. Anneke died in 1615, and two other children from their brief marriage were buried in 1613 and 1616.

Hals is recorded in 1612–15 as a musketeer in a new company of the Saint George civic guard, and from 1615 until 1624 he served in another company of the same organization. From 1616 until 1624 he was also a "friend" or "second member" of a Haarlem chamber of rhetoric, or amateur dramatic society, De Wijngaardranken (The Vine Tendrils). One of Hals's earliest known works is the portrait, dated 1616, of a *rederijker*, or rhetorician, from Leiden, Pieter Cornelisz van der Morsch (fig. 7). Van der Morsch served as beadle in the city government and as the fool in performances by the Leiden chamber of rhetoric, De Witte Accoleijen (The White Columbines). It is known from a book of verses by Van der Morsch himself that he "handed out smoked herrings," a slang expression for putting people down with sharp remarks. Fish basket at the ready, Van der Morsch inquires, "Wie begeert" (Who's asking for it?).

Also dated 1616 is Hals's first major commission, a group portrait of the Saint

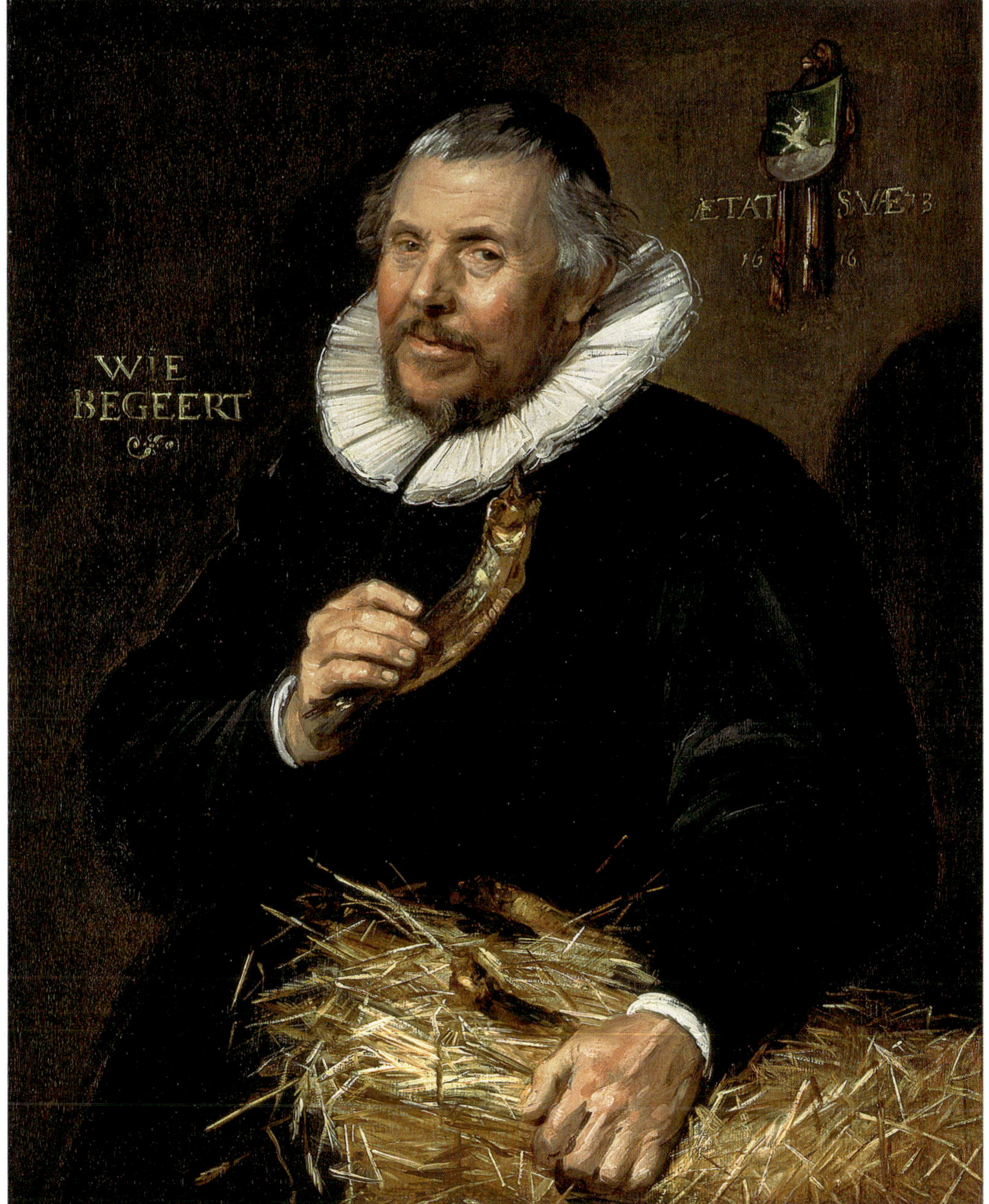

7. Frans Hals. *Pieter Cornelisz van der Morsch*, 1616. Oil on canvas, transferred from wood; 34¾ x 27⅜ in. (88.1 x 69.5 cm). Carnegie Museum of Art, Pittsburgh; Acquired through the generosity of Mrs. Alan M. Scaife (61.42.2). Van der Morsch was a Leiden civil servant and member of a chamber of rhetoric. His comic specialty was the personal insult.

George civic guard officers (fig. 8). The gentlemen recorded in this large canvas were leading citizens of Haarlem and Hals's own superiors in the company. Considering the picture's "assured execution" (not surprising for an artist in his thirties), Dutch specialists Koos Levy-van Halm and Liesbeth Abraham have wondered whether Hals "was already familiar with working to a large format."[10] What is new here, however, is not the rendering of figures on a fairly large scale but their dramatic interaction. Perhaps this is what the authors meant, since they cite the Calivermen civic guard portrait of 1599 by Cornelis Cornelisz van Haarlem (fig. 9) as Hals's "point of departure." The comparison of these compositions, and the older artist's lively portrait of the same civic guard, dated 1583, has been rehashed often by commentators (helpfully, all three works are in the Frans Hals Museum). The conventional analysis notes how naturalistically Hals relates the individual figures to each other, in contrast to Cornelisz van Haarlem's gathering of taciturn types (like strangers sharing an elevator) in his picture of 1599. In his panoramic survey of Dutch painting Slive

8. Frans Hals. *Banquet of the Officers of the Saint George Civic Guard*, 1616. Oil on canvas, 68⅞ x 127½ in. (175 x 324 cm). Frans Hals Museum, Haarlem (OS I-109). This large group portrait was Hals's first important commission, and it led to several others from Haarlem civic guard companies. Although nominally militias, these companies were essentially social organizations in which the officers were prominent citizens.

9. Cornelis Cornelisz van Haarlem (Netherlandish, Haarlem 1562–1638 Haarlem). *Banquet of the Officers and Sub-alterns of the Haarlem Calivermen Civic Guard*, 1599. Oil on canvas, 66½ x 88 in. (169 x 223.5 cm). Frans Hals Museum, Haarlem (OS I-53). The composition is much less animated than Cornelisz van Haarlem's portrait of the same company dated 1583 and has been criticized accordingly by most modern scholars. This group portrait was the first, however, to arrange the figures in a hierarchal order of rank, which could lead to prestigious appointments in city government. Here the dean, flanked by the provost and oldest captain, sits under the baldachin to the left.

describes the differences in terms of period styles, observing that "Renaissance coordination of individual parts has given way to Baroque integration."[11] Of course, the term "Baroque" (which many writers on Dutch art carefully avoid) implies participation in a stylistic movement that swept up from Italy to the art centers of northern Europe (and over to Spain). Yet at the same time Slive insists upon Hals's independence from other artists, a concept that recalls Van Mander's (1603) and Bellori's (1672) biographies of Caravaggio, which claim that the revolutionary artist recognized no master other than nature.[12] (Shakespeare was also described as a "natural" artist, owing nothing to learning, within fifteen years of his death in 1616, and the stereotype lasted until recently.)[13] Hals's first group portrait, according to Slive, "announces the golden age of Dutch painting like a cannon shot. The search for its sources . . . has been fruitless, a helpful reminder that the hunt for influences in the work of a great master can be a will-o'-the-wisp."[14]

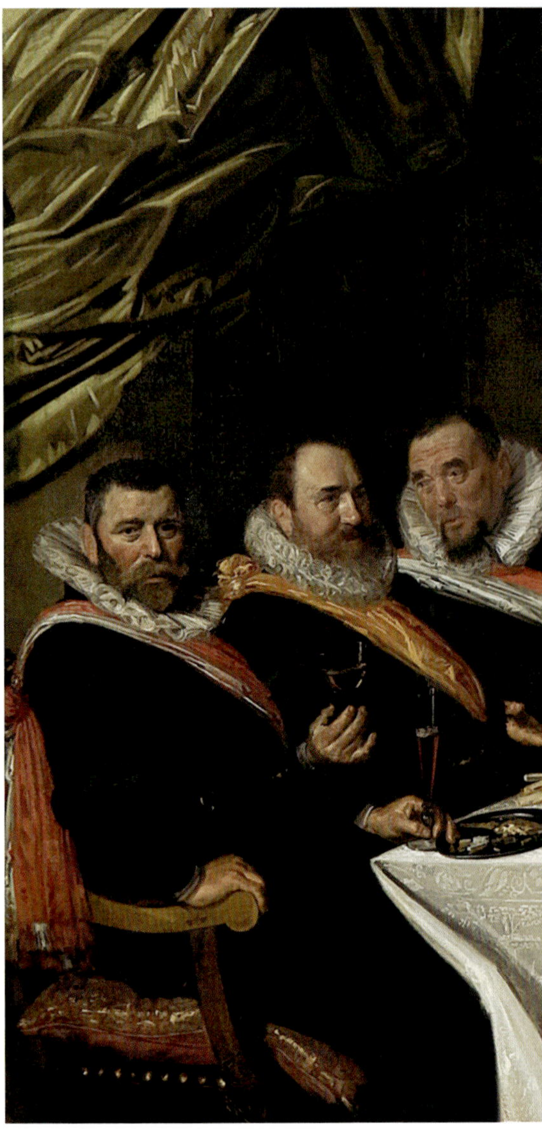

What is often found in the early works of great masters like Rembrandt, Vermeer, and Hals is the eager pursuit of so many artistic ideas that identifying particular "sources" tends to miss the point, which is the acquirement of pictorial literacy. Any pupil or reader of Van Mander would have learned how the most esteemed Dutch painters of the day had benefited from studying in Rome, Venice, Paris, Antwerp, or another cultural capital, as well as from attending to Nature and to the most accomplished masters of the Netherlandish past (such as Haarlem's own Marten van Heemskerck, who worked in Rome during the 1530s). Van Mander, who according to his own account had imported the late Mannerist style to Haarlem in the form of drawings by Bartholomeus Spranger (1546–1611), recorded approvingly in the *Schilder-Boeck* that in Italy his colleague Hendrick Goltzius turned from Spranger's example to the antique and to models such as Raphael, Correggio, Veronese, and Titian. He also related that the Amsterdam master Dirck Barendsz "brought back to the Netherlands the proper manner of Italy pure and unmixed," which he learned from his years in the circle of Titian, from about 1555 to 1561.[15]

Hals never went to Italy, but he did go to Antwerp in 1616, and he was also exposed to aspects of recent Flemish art at an earlier date. In Hals's *Portrait of a Woman* (Devonshire Collection, Chatsworth House, Derbyshire, England), which has been tentatively dated about 1612–14, Slive detects "luminous flesh tints [that] recall those found in portraits by Rubens not long after his return from Italy in December 1608" and makes the same claim for the "gleaming flesh tones" in the canvas Hals painted for the Saint George civic guard (fig. 8), which records officers retiring in 1615, the probable occasion for the commission.[16] In transforming a type of group portrait from what in Cornelisz van Haarlem's picture (fig. 9) looks like a yearbook photograph into a lively banqueting scene, it obviously occurred to Hals that a perusal of earlier banquet scenes—no matter how the company was dressed or undressed—might be useful. Groups of figures indulging themselves around large tables have numerous precedents in Venice (Veronese being the most familiar maître d'), but in the North

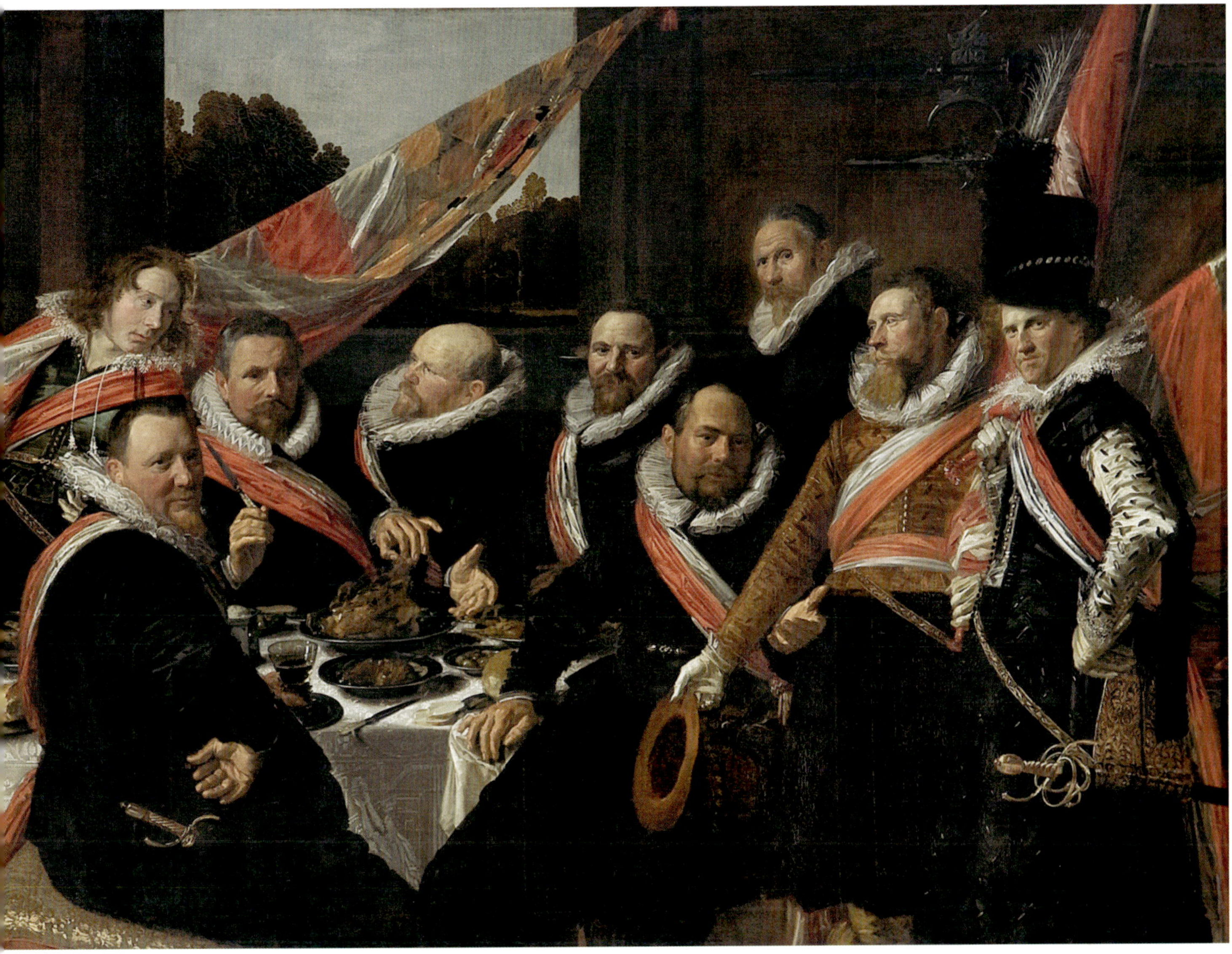

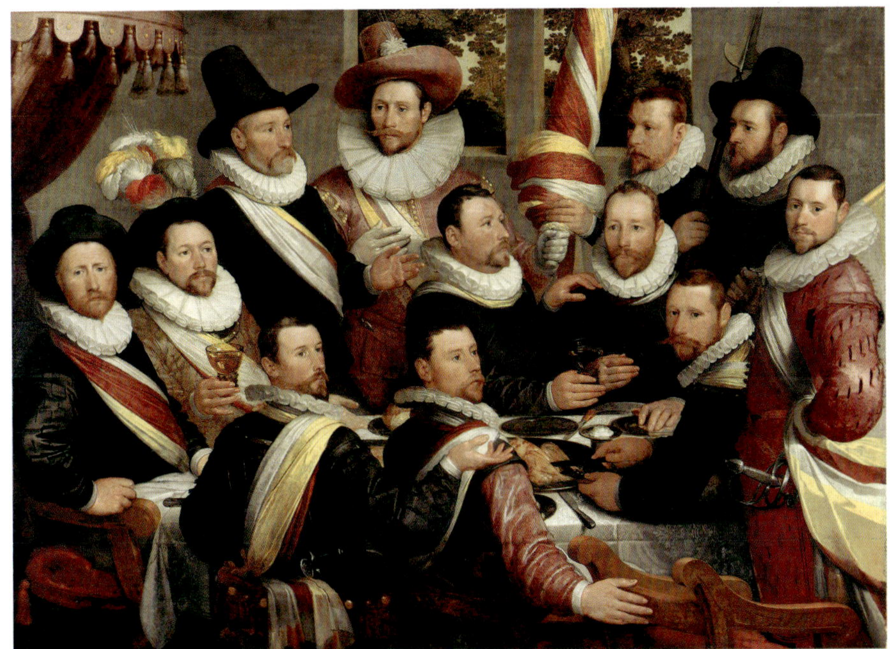

10. Anonymous engraver after Frans Floris I (Netherlandish, 1519/20–1570). *Mankind before the Flood*, 1560s (the design). Engraving, 8 x 13⅛ in. (20.4 x 33.4 cm). Museum Boijmans Van Beuningen, Rotterdam (L 1965/100 [PK]). Floris worked in Italy about 1542–45 and during the 1550s and 1560s was the most influential "Romanist" artist in his native Antwerp.

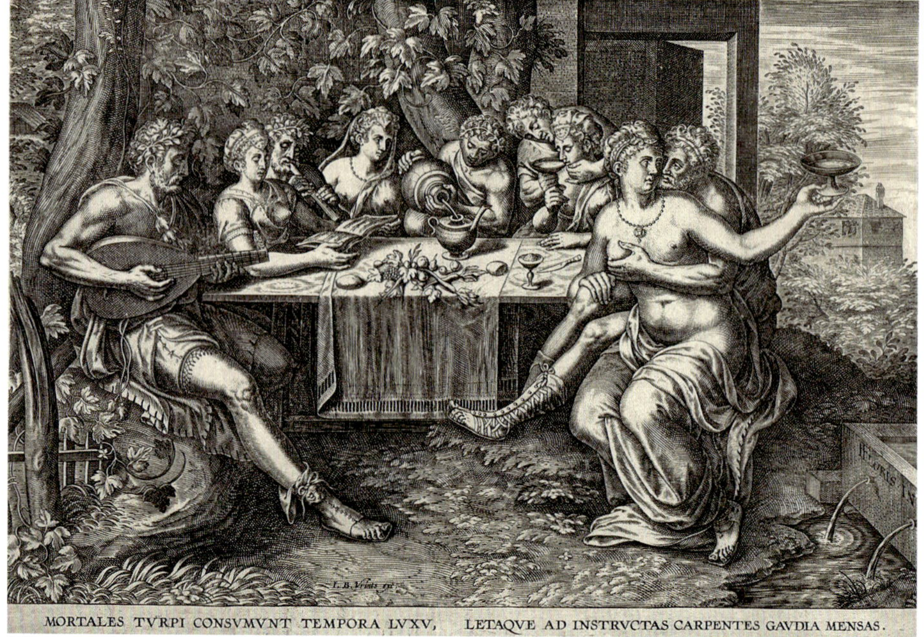

this type of composition flourished first in Antwerp, in paintings and prints by or after Frans Floris (1519/20–1570), Marten de Vos (1532–1603), Hieronymous Francken (1578–1623), Frans Francken II (1581–1624), and other artists. The fact that the figures in depictions of Feasts of the Gods, Mankind before the Flood (see fig. 10), the Wedding of Peleus and Thetis (or Cupid and Psyche), or biblical banquets ranging from Belshazzar's Feast to the Last Supper did not sport swords, sashes, or standards would not have distracted Hals from noticing how the protagonists might be seated in a loose semicircle and made to rhythmically interact. Hals's most esteemed fellow guild members, Goltzius and Cornelisz van Haarlem, were past masters in this genre and had already made the mental leap from erotic revelers like those in Goltzius's spectacular engraving after Spranger of 1587 (fig. 11) to civic guard officers like the ones Goltzius sketched in about 1600 for a painting that was never executed (fig. 12).[17]

Hals would have known many of the Flemish prototypes for his composition before 1616, since Haarlem—second only to Antwerp in print production—was well supplied with engravings after Flemish masters, some of which were made in the Dutch city. Furthermore, by the mid-1610s in Haarlem and nearby Amsterdam several artists had invented contemporary versions of the quasi-historical subjects, as in Barendsz's drawing in the manner of Veronese, *Mankind Awaiting the Last Judgment* of 1581, engraved by Jan Sadeler (fig. 13); Van Mander's *Vesper* (*Evening*), engraved by Jacob Matham in 1601; David Vinckboons's garden scene *The Prodigal Son in a Brothel*, engraved by Claes Jansz Visscher in 1608; and so on. In these popular images libidinous couples wear the latest fashions and socialize intimately à table. Paintings of similar subjects—the "Merry Companies" in which Dirck Hals was soon to specialize (see fig. 20)—were made in Haarlem at least as early as about 1614–15, by Esaias van de Velde (ca. 1590–1630) and by Willem Buytewech (1591/92–1624).[18]

None of this, however, quite prepares viewers for Frans Hals's earliest known genre scene, *Merrymakers at Shrovetide* (fig. 14), which is one of the many important Dutch paintings that Benjamin Altman left to the Metropolitan Museum at his death in 1913. The large work on canvas is usually dated about 1616 on the basis of comparisons with early works by Hals, including the portrait of Van der Morsch

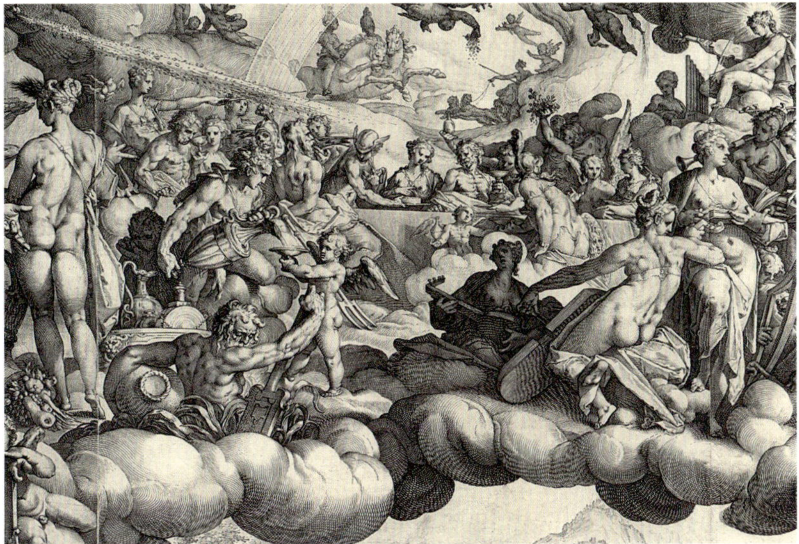

11. Hendrick Goltzius (Netherlandish, Mühlbracht 1558–1617 Haarlem) after Bartholomeus Spranger (Netherlandish, Antwerp 1546–1611 Prague). *The Wedding of Peleus and Thetis* (or *Cupid and Psyche*), 1587 (detail of center). Engraving, second state of four, printed from three plates; 17¼ x 33¾ in. (43.8 x 85.8 cm) overall. The Metropolitan Museum of Art, Purchase, The Elisha Whittelsey Collection, The Elisha Whittelsey Fund, Martha Feltenstein Gift, A. Hyatt Mayor Purchase Funds, Marjorie Phelps Starr Bequest, 2000 (2000.113). This detail shows the center background of Goltzius's famous print, about one-sixth of the entire composition. The Spranger drawing (Rijksprentenkabinet, Rijksmuseum, Amsterdam) on which it is based was inspired mainly by Raphael's fresco of the same subject in the Villa Farnesina, Rome.

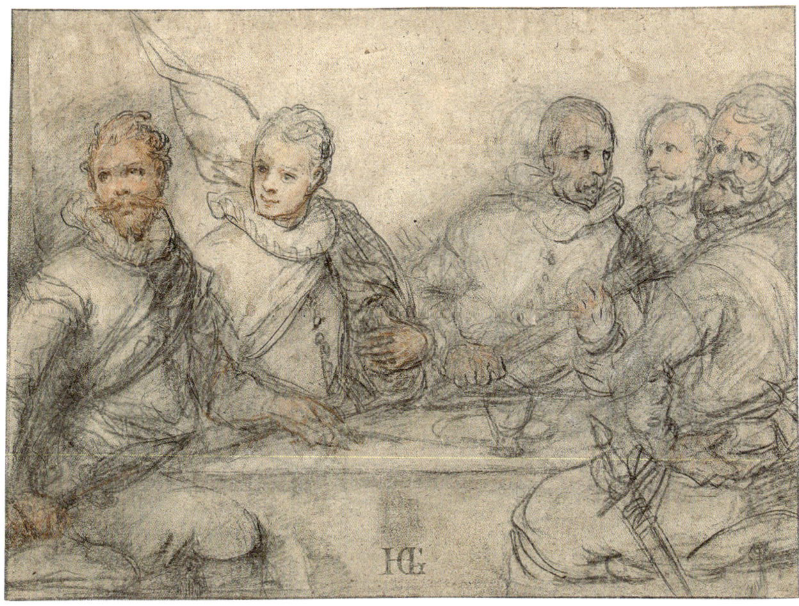

12. Hendrick Goltzius. *Five Officers, Study for a Civic Guard Portrait*, ca. 1600. Black and red chalk, washed and heightened with brush; 9½ x 12½ in. (24 x 31.8 cm). Rijksprentenkabinet, Rijksmuseum, Amsterdam (RP-T-1884-A-338). This sheet, Goltzius's only known attempt at group portraiture, is thought to be a fragment of a larger composition. The arrangement of the figures to some extent anticipates the group in the center of Hals's civic guard picture of 1616 (fig. 8).

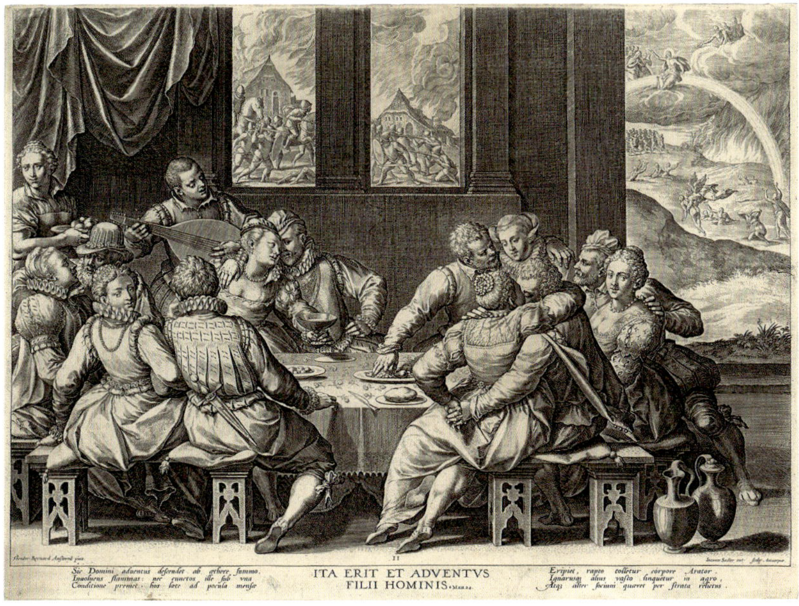

13. Jan Sadeler I (Netherlandish, Brussels 1550–1600 Venice?) after Dirck Barendsz (Netherlandish, Amsterdam 1534–1592 Amsterdam). *Mankind Awaiting the Last Judgment*, 1581. Engraving, 14⅛ x 18 in. (35.8 x 45.8 cm). The Metropolitan Museum of Art, Harris Brisbane Dick Fund, 1953 (53.601.17[52]). Like a Veronese of Amsterdam, Barendsz represented the biblical subject as a contemporary social event. The print is a pendant to the same artist's *Mankind before the Flood*, representing a similar ensemble in the nude, with a rainstorm and Noah's ark in the background. Together the Latin titles quote Matthew 24:37, in which Christ says to his disciples: "But as the days of Noah were, so shall also the coming of the Son of man be."

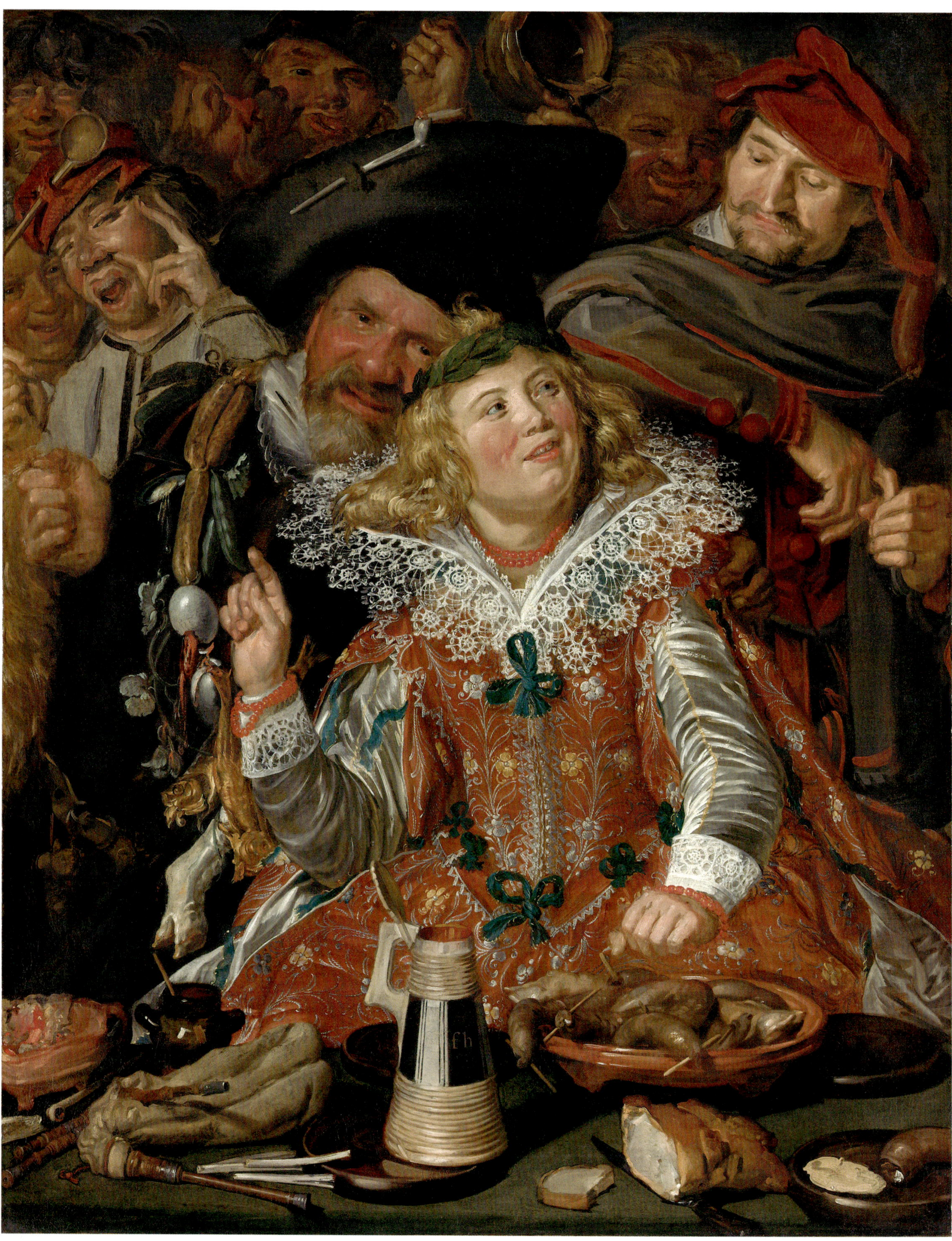
fh

(fig. 7). Claus Grimm raised the question of whether the *Merrymakers* might reflect Hals's experience in Antwerp, considering its similarities in composition and execution to contemporary works by Rubens and, especially, the young Jacob Jordaens.[19] (Jordaens never studied abroad, so Italianate ideas usually came to him after they had already been translated into a Flemish idiom. This may have made Jordaens's manner more accessible to Hals than that of Rubens or other Antwerp Italophiles, such as Abraham Janssen.) Indeed, the picture is one of the most Flemish-looking works to have been painted in Holland before the 1620s, and it is very tempting to associate its shift in style from slightly earlier paintings by Hals (such as the civic guard portrait, fig. 8) with his stay in Antwerp from some time before August 6 until the second week of November in 1616.[20] The way the crowded figures and objects on the table completely fill the frame, seeming to press against the picture plane, and are painted in broad, open brushstrokes, with bold colors and shadows rendered in tones of blue and green, recalls several early pictures by Jordaens such as *Christ Blessing the Children* of about 1615 (Saint Louis Art Museum), *Christ's Charge to Peter* of about 1616 (Church of Saint James, Antwerp), and *The Adoration of the Shepherds* of 1616 (fig. 15), which originally had yet another figure squeezed into the congested group. Placing *The Adoration of the Shepherds* next to *Merrymakers at Shrovetide* supports the hypothesis that Hals had recently been looking at works by Jordaens, although the *Adoration* is hardly the most similar picture in the Fleming's early oeuvre. In addition to the obvious correspondences in palette, brushwork, and sinuous contours, there is a less expected similarity in the treatment of broad highlights on drapery, as seen especially when the figures to the right in each picture are compared.

The commotion of colors, movement, and flashing highlights in *Merrymakers at Shrovetide* suits its subject: a carnival celebration on the eve of Lent, or Shrove Tuesday (called Vastenavond, or Fasting Eve, in the Netherlands). On such an occasion, public drinking, popular food (especially sausages), raucous instruments (such as bagpipes and rommel pots), silly costumes, and comic performances would have been the norm. Hals centered attention on a young woman with a bull neck and a laurel wreath who is flanked by two figures from the comic stage: to the left is Pekelharing (Pickled Herring), with a foxtail (symbol of fools) in his right hand, and to the right is Hans Worst (John Sausage), who greets the girl with an obscene gesture. A sausage dangles from Hans's hat, and herring are included in Pekelharing's garland, which consists also of sausages and beans (phallic forms, like fish), a mussel (the feminine counterpart), eggs (symbol of virility, except when broken), and a pig's foot (which usually alludes to gluttony). Most of the objects on the table refer to male or female parts; the limp bagpipe, for instance, would have been understood as a witty estimate of the old man's amorous

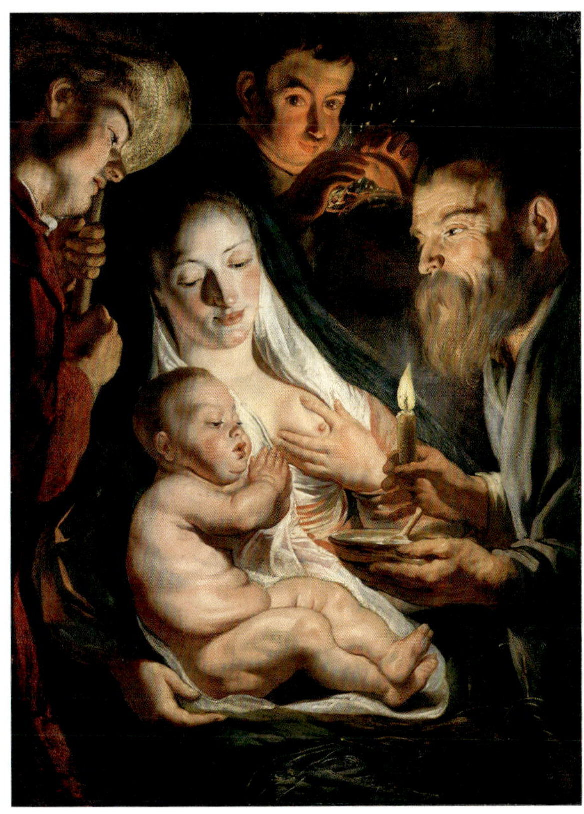

14. Frans Hals. *Merrymakers at Shrovetide*, ca. 1616. Oil on canvas, 51¾ x 39¼ in. (131.4 x 99.7 cm). The Metropolitan Museum of Art, Bequest of Benjamin Altman, 1913 (14.40.605). In America especially, collectors and dealers of Altman's day favored Hals's most dignified portraits, such as the *Paulus Verschuur* (fig. 31) from Arabella Huntington's collection (acquired by 1909). However, Altman frequently went his own way, which brought to the Museum three important genre paintings by Hals (see also figs. 18 and 42). The red dress worn by the young "woman" (all *rederijkers* were male) would have seemed typical of a Flemish floozy to Dutch eyes, although fashion excesses were a topic Hals could have studied in prints.

15. Jacob Jordaens (Flemish, Antwerp 1593–1678 Antwerp). *The Adoration of the Shepherds*, 1616. Oil on canvas, transferred from wood; 42 x 30 in. (106.7 x 76.2 cm). The Metropolitan Museum of Art, Bequest of Miss Adelaide Milton de Groot (1876–1967), 1967 (67.187.76). Even in religious and mythological paintings, Jordaens (who never went to Italy) employed everyday Netherlandish types, which may have made his colorful early works more appealing to Hals than Rubens's classicizing manner of about 1612–16.

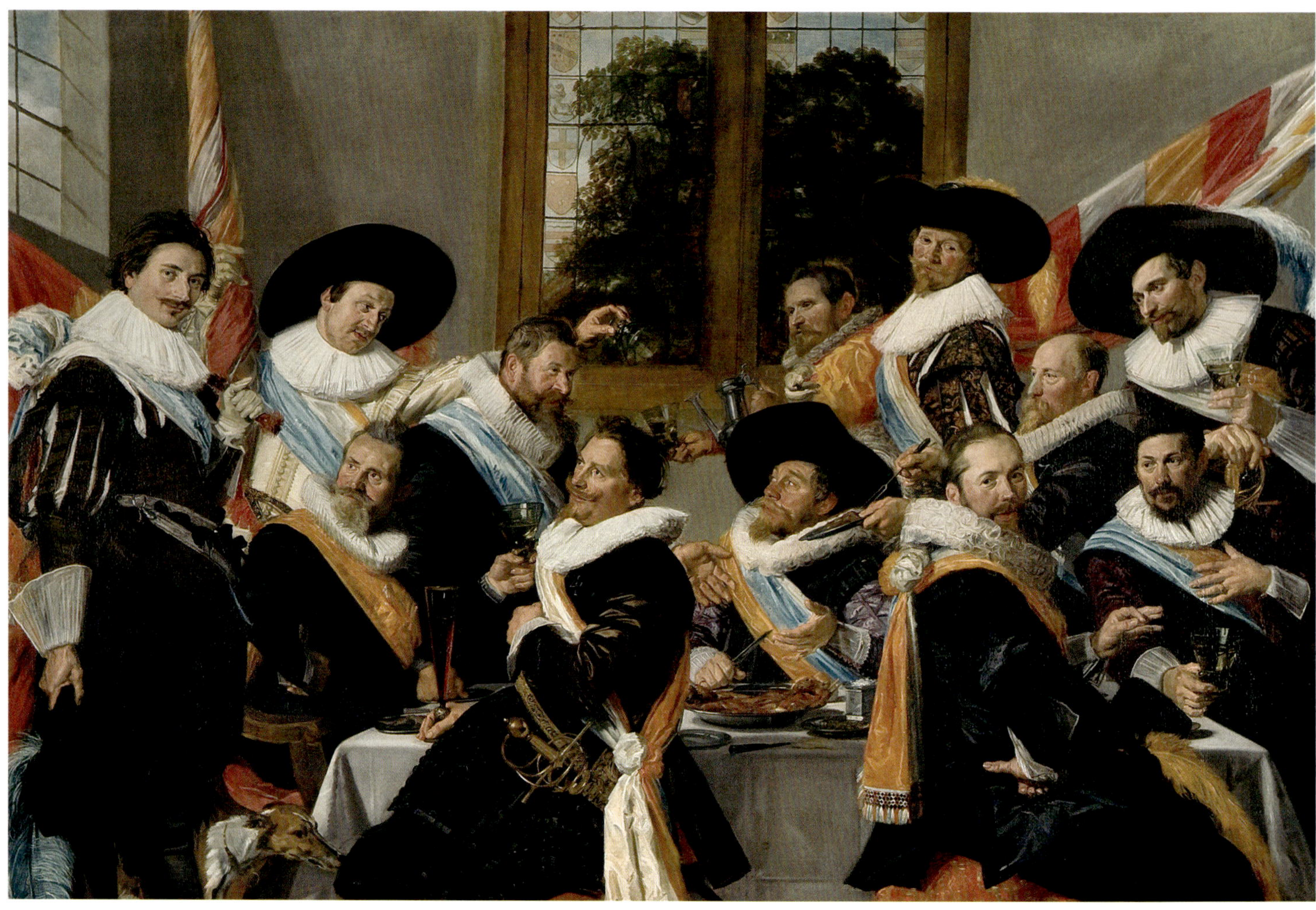

16. Frans Hals. *Banquet of the Officers of the Calivermen Civic Guard*, 1627. Oil on canvas, 73¼ x 104⅞ in. (183 x 266.5 cm). Frans Hals Museum, Haarlem (OS I-111). The company depicted has often been identified as the Saint Hadrian Civic Guard, but the title given here has recently been shown to be the correct one. As did Rembrandt in group portraits such as *The Anatomy Lesson of Dr. Tulp* of 1632 (Mauritshuis, The Hague), Hals employed compositional ideas adopted from Early Baroque history pictures to dramatize the ensemble.

potential. Such a picture would not have been intended for the average Dutch home but might have been acquired by a chamber of rhetoric or an individual *rederijker*. Indeed, one may wonder whether the canvas was painted for Pieter van der Morsch, whose portrait (fig. 7) dates from about the same time.

Merrymakers at Shrovetide is not the only painting by Hals that makes one curious about his more than three months in Antwerp, at a time when the city's art world was a cornucopia of new ideas. In 1616 Hals would have witnessed overwhelming works by Rubens (including some of his greatest altarpieces), the prolific activity of the young Jordaens, Van Dyck's prodigious debut, and paintings by Abraham Janssen, Cornelis de Vos, Frans Snyders, and several other masters who, if they were working in a Dutch city at the time, would have been counted among the most important artists in the country. The question is interesting for the two most remarkable aspects of Hals's style: his command of Early Baroque compositional schemes, which is a largely neglected topic; and his famous brushwork, which has been more successfully described than explained.

Hals's works of the 1620s make clear that he was conversant in an international language: the words, so to speak, are Dutch, but the syntax may be traced back to cosmopolitan masters such as Rubens and ultimately to Italy. Hals's most animated group portrait, the Calivermen civic guard picture of 1627 (fig. 16), is organized on a broad X-pattern, with two groups of figures converging like wedges from either side, the kind of encounter one finds in Rubens's *Abraham and Melchizedek* of about 1615 (fig. 17) and in other grand history pictures by him dating from the late 1610s and 1620s. *Boy with a Lute* of about 1625 (fig. 42) and similar pictures by Hals are usually seen as indebted to the Utrecht Caravaggist Gerrit van Honthorst (1592–1656); its dramatic type of pose, which was introduced by Caravaggio in Rome, had become fairly common currency in the Northern and Spanish Netherlands, if not yet in Haarlem, by the time Hals adopted it.

The hero (or antihero) of Hals's *Young Man and Woman in an Inn*, dated 1623 (fig. 18), also recalls works by Van Honthorst, such as the *Merry Violinist with a Wineglass* of the same year (Rijksmuseum, Amsterdam), but his pose and the viewer's low vantage point make the figure appear heroic in a manner found not in Utrecht but in Antwerp and Rome. (Bernini's *Saint Longinus* comes to mind, although that sculpture in Saint Peter's dates from the next decade and is focused on something higher than an upraised glass.) A good number of figures by Rubens, usually holding lances (martial saints, risen Christs, and Adonis embraced by Venus in the passionate nude scene of about 1610 in the Museum Kunstpalast, Düsseldorf), are presented similarly. Hals was clever enough to splice in a background based on Flemish kitchen interiors, which were also adopted in Utrecht, by Joachim Wtewael, at about the same time.[21] And yet the whole arrangement looks so immediate in Hals's handling that it seems as if a door has just been flung open and the happy couple are about to fall over the viewer or down a flight of steps.

Hals's debt to and distance from the Netherlandish past may be measured by comparing *Young Man and Woman in an Inn* with a picture of nearly the same subject by the Antwerp painter Jan van Hemessen (fig. 19). Cropping the older composition would isolate the man and his pretty companion, as in Hals's painting, and likewise place the actors at the front of their stage. But Van Hemessen's viewpoint is high, his figures are stiffly sculptural, and the spatial effect of the whole is fragmented, with background vignettes added like explanatory notes in the margins of a text. By contrast, Hals's inn scene is all of a piece; the viewer takes it in as if drawing a breath. Of course, the design could be picked apart in a classroom, for example by noting how the long diagonal recession from the rake's highlighted elbow back to the innkeeper is countered by the thrusting attentions of the girl and the dog, and how the couple's heads are framed not only by his hat and her collar but also by the blue brackets formed by his sleeve and oversized feather (something no sensible Dutchman would ever wear). But when one stands in front of the picture its artificial elements are swept away by a wave of sensations: light, air, movement, and, one imagines, taste, smell, and noise.

In his handling of an old subject Hals also put new wine in a new bottle. In this he was not alone: Van Honthorst and other Utrecht painters depicted carousing young men reminiscent of the Prodigal Son, although none of these pictures (nor even Van Hemessen's) is thought to illustrate the passage in the Gospel of Luke. A Dutch play published in 1630 by Willem Dircksz

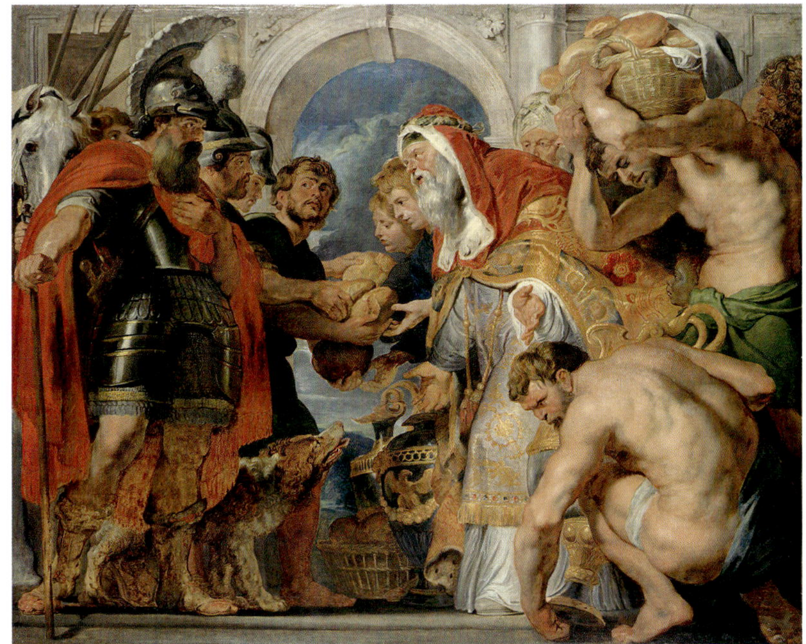

17. Peter Paul Rubens (Flemish, Siegen 1577–1640 Antwerp). *Abraham and Melchizedek*, ca. 1615. Oil on canvas, 80¼ x 98⅜ in. (204 x 250 cm). Musée des Beaux-Arts de Caen (172)

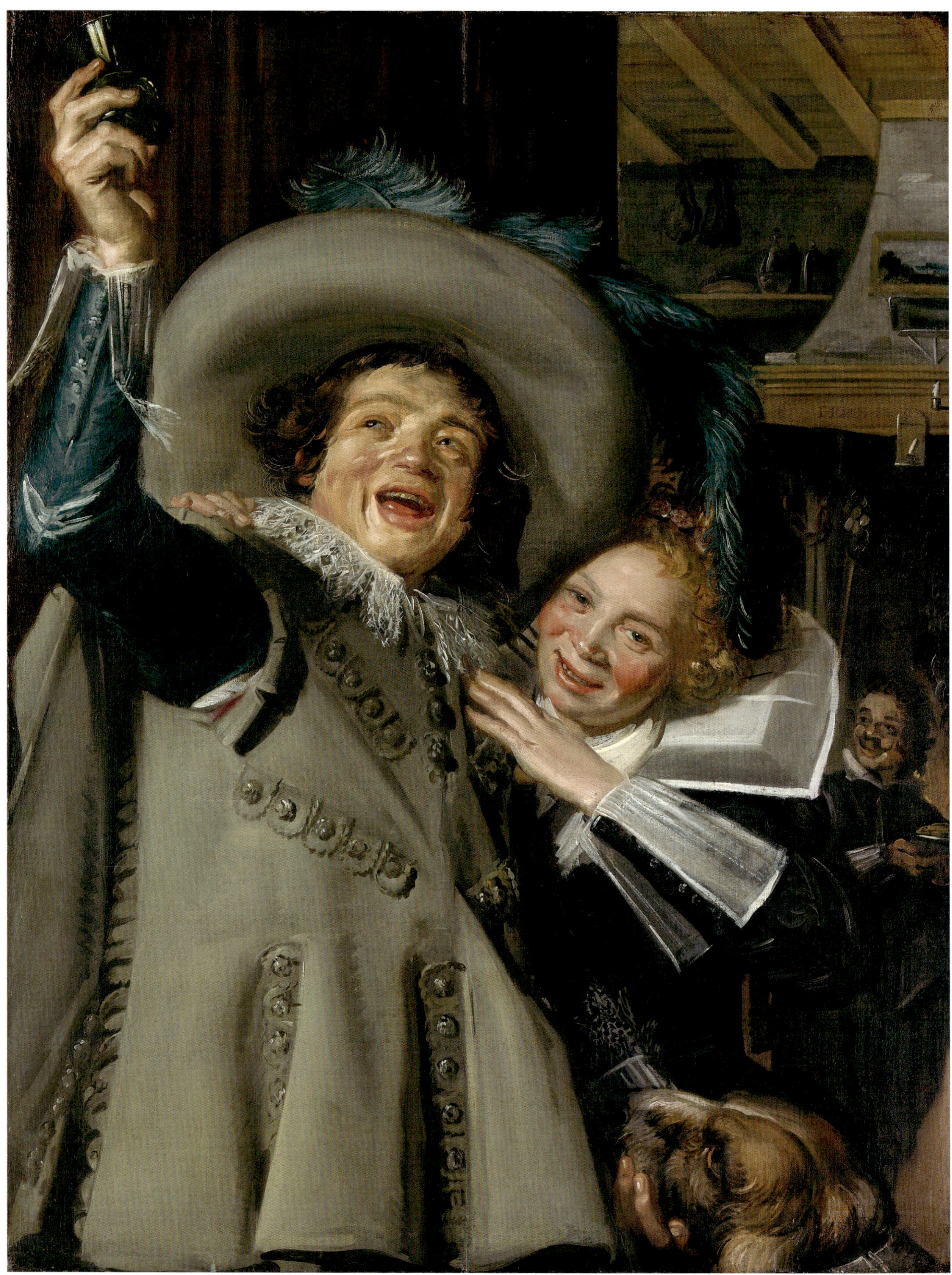

Hooft bears the telling title *Heden-daeghsche Verlooren Soon* (Present-day Prodigal Son) and on the title page shows a dandy waving his wine glass overhead while a prostitute strokes his chin and a procuress steals his purse. Hals certainly would have known the much finer engraving by Gillis van Breen after Van Mander (1597), which shows a similar trio in a tavern with a pair of dogs leaping up for the treat in the wastrel's hand. At the bottom of the print an inscription reads in Italian and a Dutch translation: "The nuzzle of dogs, the love of whores, the hospitality of innkeepers: None of it comes without cost."[22] Less concise essays on the same theme were painted by Hals's brother Dirck (see fig. 20) and other Haarlem artists in the 1620s. The subject of modern youth wasting their parents' money on worldly pleasures would have gone down well with Hals's contemporaries in Haarlem, since many of them had suffered from Spanish oppression and economic hardship before flourishing in the north. In that respect, the period of the Twelve Years' Truce (1609–21) in Holland is analogous to America's postwar era of Eisenhower and Elvis.

Most or all of Hals's iconographic ideas could have been picked up in Haarlem, from prints, publications (such as emblem books, which were compilations of symbolic pictures with commentary in verse and prose), and other artists. There was such a strong tradition of learning among the city's most celebrated masters—Van Heemskerck, his intellectual printmaker Dirck Volkertsz Coornhert, and the latter's pupil Goltzius, as well as Van Mander and others—that it is hardly surprising to find Hals (despite Houbraken's image of him) deftly dealing with subjects and symbols derived from a variety of literary sources. A well-known example is the large canvas of about 1622, *A Married Couple in a Garden (Isaac Massa and Beatrix van der Laen?)*, in the Rijksmuseum, Amsterdam, which is rich in marriage symbolism. Slive suggests that "aspects of its iconographical programme" may have been recalled from Rubens's *Self-portrait with Isabella Brandt in a Honeysuckle Bower* of about 1609–10 (Bayerische Staatsgemäldesammlungen, Munich). But if Hals saw that painting in Antwerp (in Rubens's own house), "he must have firmly resolved that no one would ever accuse him of plagiarising the pictorial organisation" of that almost equally accessible and charming work.[23] In fact, similar compositions (a couple set off to the side in a diagonally receding landscape) had already been employed in other works by Rubens (and a few by Jordaens), and had any critics noticed the connection at the time they would have been less inclined to blame Hals for emulating Rubens than to congratulate him.

No evidence suggests that Hals went to Antwerp for some reason other than to study works of art in the cultural capital of the Netherlands. (It is also quite possible that he had been there before, considering the scarcity of documents dating from before May 31, 1615, when his wife was buried.) In 1616 the painter had just completed his first big project (fig. 8), which probably brought him enough income to travel and to temporarily defer other earnings. Money

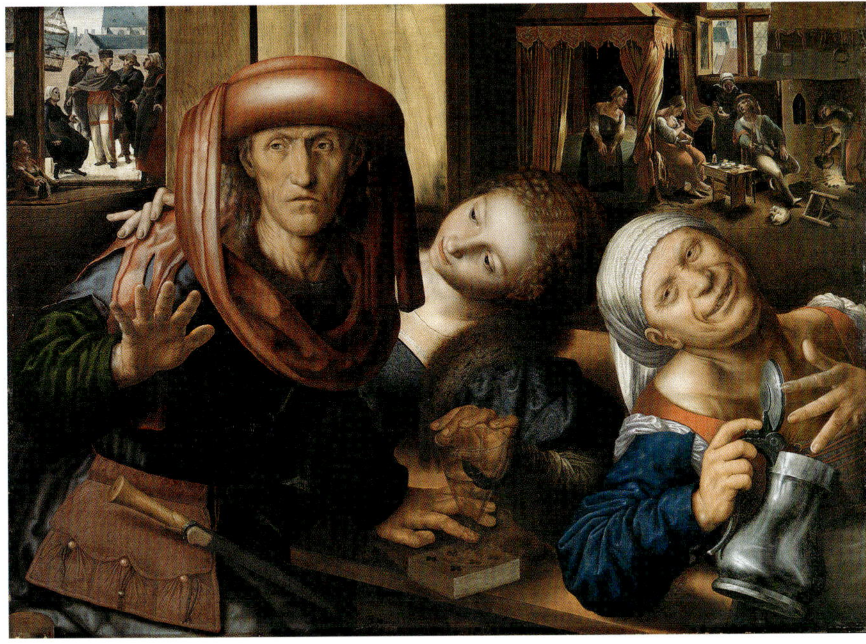

18. Frans Hals. *Young Man and Woman in an Inn ("Yonker Ramp and His Sweetheart")*, 1623. Oil on canvas, 41½ x 31¼ in. (105.4 x 79.4 cm). The Metropolitan Museum of Art, Bequest of Benjamin Altman, 1913 (14.40.602). This large picture, Hals's only genre scene to bear a date, was given its popular title in the eighteenth century. It was mistakenly thought that the carousing young man was Pieter Ramp, who holds the flag in the right background of fig. 16.

19. Jan Sanders van Hemessen (Netherlandish, active Antwerp 1519–56). *Merry Company*, 1530s. Oil on wood, 32⅝ x 43⅞ in. (83 x 111.5 cm). Staatliche Kunsthalle Karlsruhe (152)

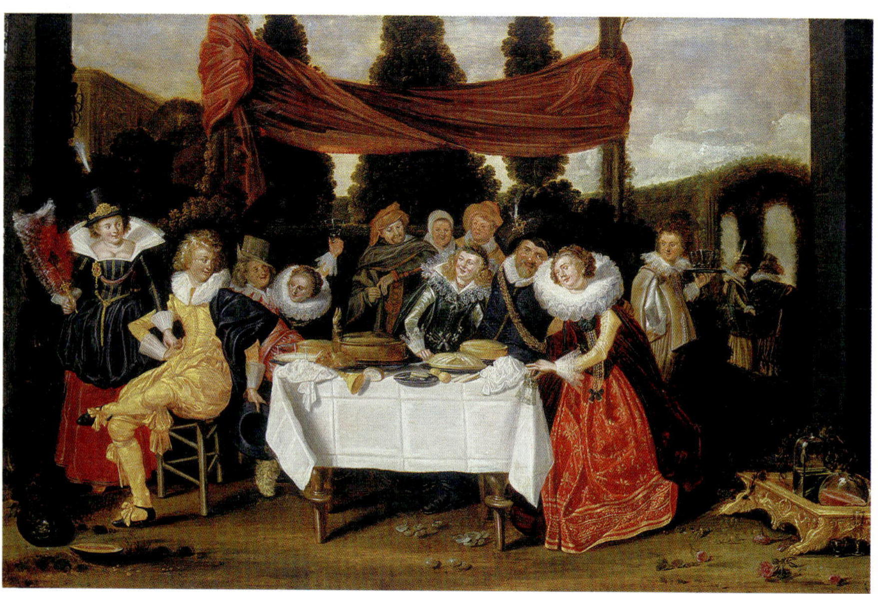

20. Dirck Hals (Dutch, Haarlem 1591–1656 Haarlem). *Merry Company*, ca. 1620. Oil on wood, 19¼ x 28¾ in. (49 x 73 cm). Städel Museum, Frankfurt am Main (20307). The young woman in blue at the table and the men to either side of her are based on the main figures in Frans Hals's *Merrymakers at Shrovetide* (fig. 14).

21. Hendrick Goltzius. *The Fall of Man*, 1616. Oil on canvas, 41¾ x 55⅛ in. (106 x 140 cm). National Gallery of Art, Washington, Patrons' Permanent Fund (1996.34.1). The warm tonality of the well-modeled figures and their friezelike arrangement in the foreground recall then recent works by Rubens, such as *Jupiter and Callisto*, 1613 (Staatliches Museum, Schwerin).

to pay the woman who cared for his two children during his absence (which only one of them survived) came directly from the treasurer of the civic guard.[24] Three months after his return to Haarlem, on February 12, 1617, Hals married Lysbeth Reyniersdr, who between that year and 1634 bore at least eleven children. The artist rarely left town again.

Rubens had been very much on the minds of Haarlem artists since his visit there in June 1612. The main purpose of his trip to the province of Holland was to find skilled engravers to reproduce his designs, and he found them in Goltzius's stepson and closest collaborator, Jacob Matham, who engraved Rubens's great *Samson and Delilah* (1609–10; National Gallery, London) in 1613; in Buytewech, who etched works by Rubens in the same year; in Jan Muller, who reproduced princely portraits by Rubens in 1615; and in the young Pieter Soutman, who made prints after Rubens in the 1620s and later on.

The example of Rubens was important also for the leading artist in Haarlem, Goltzius, in the pictures he painted from about 1613 through 1616. Until recently, one could hardly read a word on the subject because of a long-standing schism in the specialized literature between Dutch and Flemish art (something the first author in the field, Van Mander, would not have comprehended), and because if any location in the Netherlands was home to the rise of naturalistic representation—as opposed, in some minds, to artistic learning—it was surely Haarlem, with its "pioneering" landscape, marine, still life, genre, and portrait painters. In the eyes of those artists, however, Goltzius (who took up painting in 1600, after a career as Europe's greatest living engraver) would have been the grand old man of the painters' guild, and Hals would have been impressed that Goltzius's large history pictures, mostly with nude figures (as in fig. 21), were inspired in part by the famous Fleming who was only five years older than Hals himself.[25] Rubens's effect on Goltzius was certainly noted by Soutman, who in about 1616 set off for Antwerp to train as a painter with Rubens (he served as one of his studio assistants for about eight years).[26] Two years later Pieter de Grebber stayed in Antwerp with his father, the Haarlem painter and art dealer Frans Pietersz de Grebber, who served as Rubens's agent in business with the English ambassador at The Hague, Sir Dudley Carleton. Rubens was important for the younger De Grebber's work in Haarlem during the 1620s.[27]

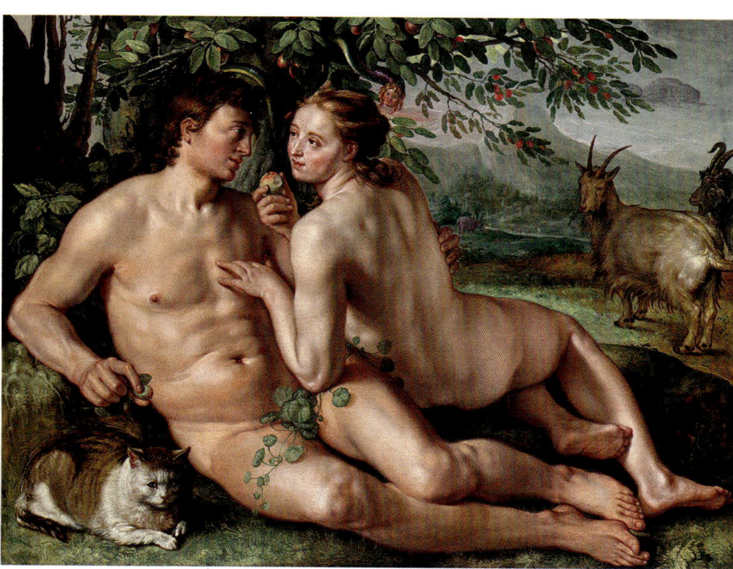

But unlike Soutman and De Grebber and a few other artists of the younger generation in Haarlem, such as Salomon de Bray, Hals evidently never had any ambition to follow Goltzius's practice, and Van Mander's advice, by painting history pictures. Perhaps as a consequence, the influence of Rubens is not very clear in Hals's work, apart from some rather general qualities of composition and execution. Once in Antwerp, to which Rubens's reputation would have drawn him, Hals appears to have responded mainly to Jordaens (who was twenty-three at the time) and perhaps also to Van Dyck (who was only seventeen). In addition to Jordaens's early paintings of figure groups (no matter their subject type), Hals most likely focused on the "study heads" (as they are now known) that had recently been painted by Rubens, Jordaens, and possibly Van Dyck. Of all the examples that may be dated in or before 1616, those by Jordaens are the most interesting for Hals because of their fluid and forceful brushwork. Although these oil studies (fig. 22, for instance) were often used as models for figures in history pictures, they usually depicted real people from the artist's milieu, chosen because of their suitable features or sense of character. Together with ways of posing portrait subjects, for which the Antwerp masters had a special flair, the painterly description of live models in Flemish study heads must have been among Hals's most lasting impressions from the months he spent in the Spanish Netherlands.[28]

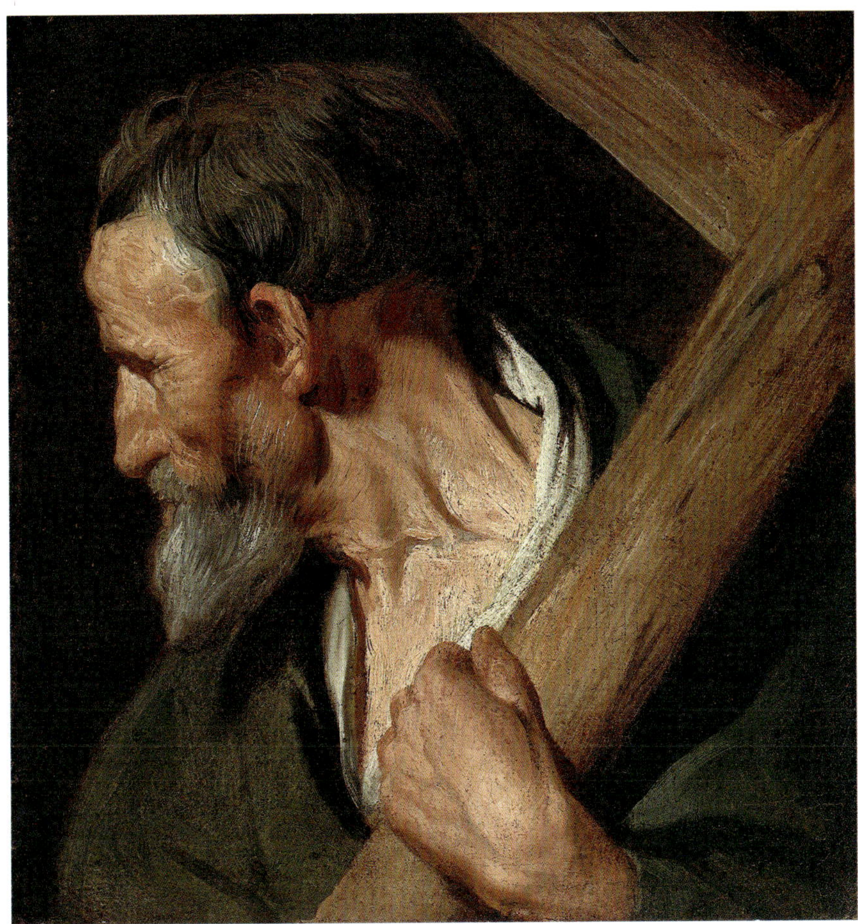

22. Jacob Jordaens. *Saint Andrew*, ca. 1618–20. Oil on canvas, 21½ x 19⅝ in. (54.6 x 49.8 cm). Private collection. Similar "study heads" were painted by Jordaens as early as about 1615–16.

Of course, artists tend to see what they are looking for; it would be a mistake to discover the seeds of Hals's distinctive style solely in Flemish soil. His earliest works reveal evidence to the contrary, for example in the treatment of the sitter's hair, the linen collar and cuffs, the *vanitas* attribute of a skull, and several bright highlights (especially on the gesturing hand) in *Portrait of a Man Holding a Skull*, probably painted in about 1612 (Barber Institute of Fine Arts, University of Birmingham). Christopher Atkins, in an article on Hals's "virtuoso brushwork," relates the artist's loose or "rough" (*rouw*) handling to his teacher Van Mander's comparison of two distinct manners, the *rouw* and the *net* (neat), and his beatification of Titian as the patron saint of the first and (he cautions) more difficult approach.[29] (Van Mander praised Dirck Barendsz for his allegedly Titianesque technique; see fig. 23). Despite these antecedents, however, Atkins concludes that "roughly treated passages" first appear in Hals's early portrait of Pieter Cornelisz van der Morsch of 1616 (fig. 7) and that the artist's painterly style first emerged as a consistent approach in the genre paintings of the 1620s (such as figs. 18, 24, 42).[30] He considers one of Van Dyck's study heads (one of five in the Alte Pinakothek, Munich), which he dates to about 1616, as a source of inspiration, but also compares a drawing by Goltzius.[31] (The artist's chiaroscuro woodcuts, with their thick black lines, separately printed colors,

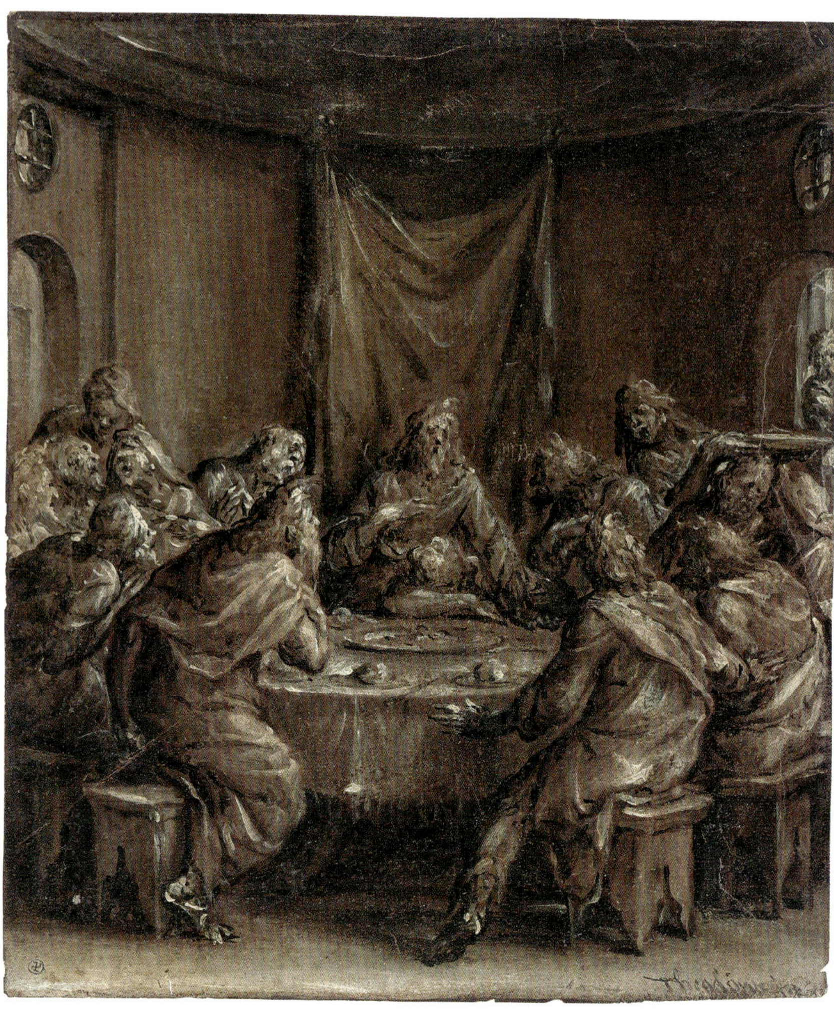

23. Dirck Barendsz (Netherlandish, Amsterdam 1534–1592 Amsterdam). *The Last Supper*, ca. 1575–85. Oil on paper, 9⅝ x 8 in. (24.5 x 20.4 cm). Rijksmuseum, Amsterdam (RP-T-1995-8). This painterly oil sketch by the Titian follower Barendsz (who worked in his native Amsterdam from about 1562 to 1592) is one of forty grisaille models for a series of engravings representing the Passion of Christ.

and bright white highlights, seem even more relevant to Hals.) The most helpful point of Atkins's essay, for modern viewers who might describe the artist as "ahead of his time," is that Hals's painterly style was regarded by his contemporaries—not only by his nineteenth-century "discoverers" and later enthusiasts—as a display of technical virtuosity, with its own critical history and an appreciative audience in collectors such as Nicolaes Duyst van Voorhout (fig. 5). In 1636 the Amsterdam lawyer and poet Johannes van Heemskerck wrote in a personal letter that he tried to write with an "able fluency," because "neat rhymes, elaborated in velvety little words [are] devoid of any spirit or life." He compared the fastidious approach to writing with "those old master paintings of the last century" in the Netherlands, which he considered less pleasing than "the works of artists of our time, though [they are] designed with a rougher brush and a more robust handling."[32]

Portraits had a very different purpose than genre scenes, namely to preserve the appearance of the sitter (often on an important occasion, such as marriage) for his or her family and to suggest social standing through costume, pose, and even expression. Artistic qualities were generally a secondary consideration, to the extent that very often only the sitter and not the painter would be identified in contemporary inventories (including those otherwise filled with artists' names). The 1657 inventory of the collection of Floris Soop, for example, refers to the Metropolitan Museum's great portrait of him by Rembrandt and to three portraits by Hals that Soop is known to have owned, but the names of those two already renowned masters are not recorded.[33]

In a genre picture like *The Smoker* (fig. 24), by contrast, Hals was working on speculation, not commission, and the painting (in addition to treating a topical subject) was intended as a demonstration of dazzling technique. The composition, crowded into an octagonal format (the wood panel's original shape), could be described as a simplified version of the main figures in *Young Man and Woman in an Inn* (fig. 18). But now the couple is much closer to the viewer, and the execution differs accordingly. In comparing the two paintings, which date from 1623 and about 1625, it might be allowed that the smaller work was probably painted more quickly, as an inexpensive item for the open market, and that the wood support accounts in good part for the slicker appearance of the loose brushwork (an effect that Hals exploited especially in the smoker's slashed doublet and in the play of light on his face). The young man's face and hair have a stronger sense of form and texture than is found in his companion's head and lace collar, while the waitress in the background is just a quick sketch.

Comparing the three figures with each other or with counterparts in other works

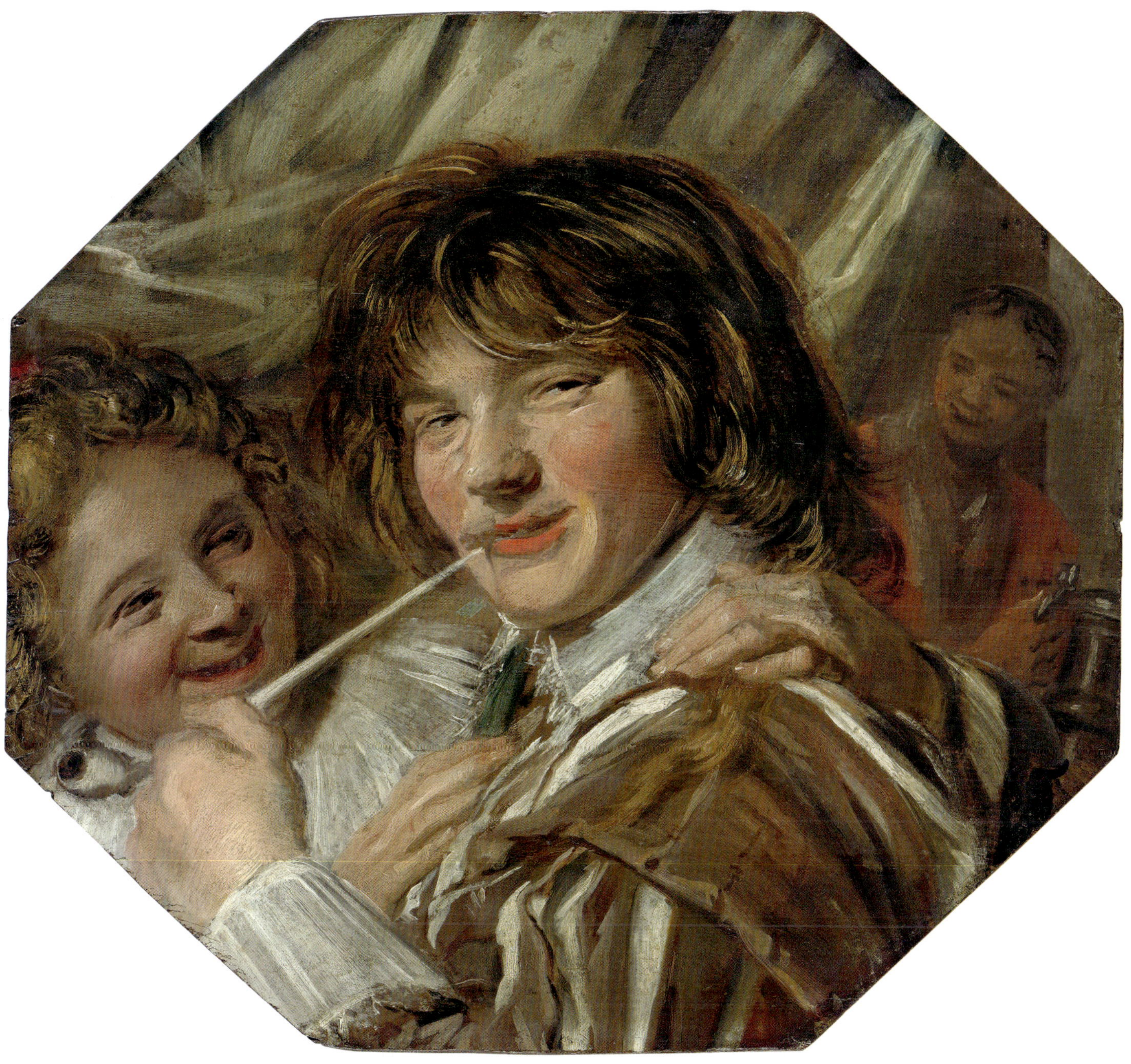

by Hals (for example, the girl and innkeeper in fig. 18) could lead one to the erroneous conclusion (as it did Grimm) that one or both of the subordinate figures in *The Smoker* might have been painted by a pupil or hypothetical assistant of Hals.[34] But stepping back to a normal viewing distance (Grimm favors tight details) and consulting Van Mander helps to clarify what Hals did with the whole. Picking up the point from Vasari's life of Titian (1568), Van Mander observed that late works by the Venetian master were meant to be seen from a certain distance. And about sixty years later Cornelis de Bie, in his "Golden Cabinet" on the art of painting, was probably recalling Van Mander when he described Hals as "still living in Haarlem, [and still] a marvel at painting portraits or counterfeits which appear very rough and bold, nimbly touched and well composed, pleasing and ingenious, and when seen from a distance seem to lack nothing but life itself."[35]

Dutch commentators borrowed many ideas from their Italian counterparts and like them repeated opinions that were

24. Frans Hals. *The Smoker*, ca. 1625. Oil on wood (octagonal), 18⅜ x 19½ in. (46.7 x 49.5 cm). The Metropolitan Museum of Art, Marquand Collection, Gift of Henry G. Marquand, 1889 (89.15.34). Prints of the period often show smokers in taverns or bordellos. An engraving after Dirck Hals compares the new fad of tobacco with "indecent lovemaking" and claims that while both corrupt the soul, smoking is also bad for the body.

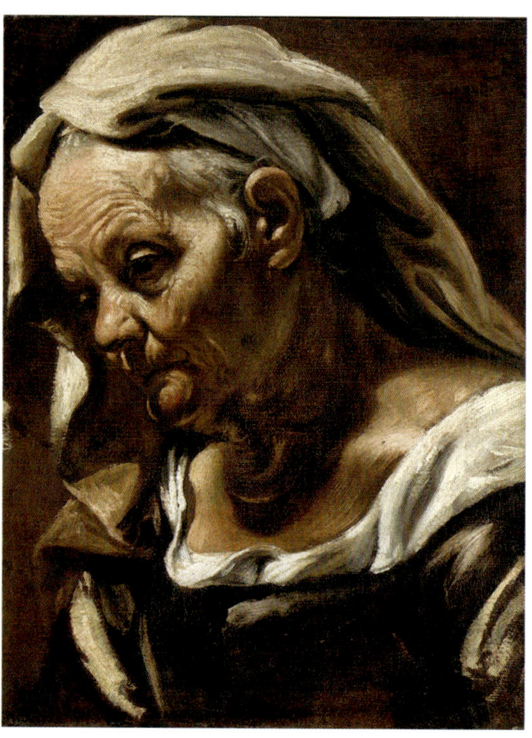

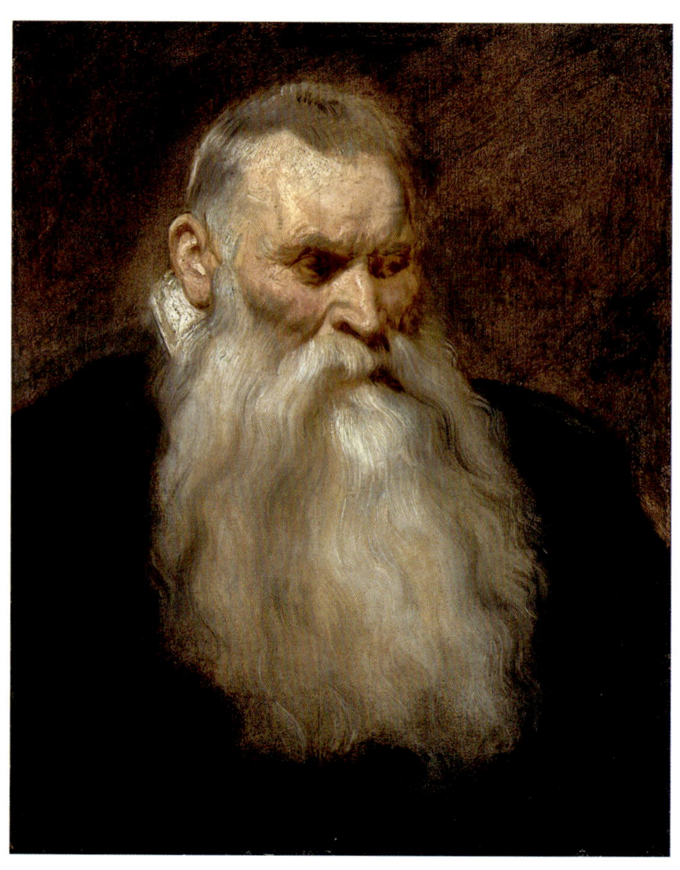

25. Orazio Borgianni (Italian, Rome 1574–1616 Rome). *Head of an Old Woman*, ca. 1612–15. Oil on canvas, 20⅞ x 15⅜ in. (53 x 39 cm). The Metropolitan Museum of Art, Purchase, Gwynne Andrews Fund and Marco Voena and Luigi Koelliker Gift, 2010 (2010.289)

26. Anthony van Dyck (Flemish, Antwerp 1599–1641 London). *Study Head of an Old Man with a White Beard*, ca. 1618. Oil on wood, 26 x 20¼ in. (66 x 51.5 cm). The Metropolitan Museum of Art, Egleston Fund, 1922 (22.221)

current in studios. De Bie's remark about Hals's "rough and bold" brushwork lending life to his figures brings to mind not only the usual praise of Titian but also contemporary criticism of Caravaggio. As early as 1617–21 the connoisseur and soon-to-be papal physician Giulio Mancini commended Caravaggio as the head of a modern school but criticized his dependence on nature and, more intriguingly, his "unnatural" light and the (likewise?) frozen look of his figures: "Especially in narrative compositions and in the suggestion of emotions, which are based on imagination and not on the direct observation of things, mere copying does not seem to me satisfactory since it is impossible to place in a room a group of people acting out a story, with light coming in from a single window, having to laugh, cry, or pretend to walk while staying still in order to be copied. As a result, the features, though they appear forceful, lack movement, expression, and grace."[36] In 1672 Bellori also spoke of inadequate composition and "movements" in Caravaggio's *Martyrdom of Saint Matthew* (San Luigi dei Francesi, Rome).[37]

My colleague Keith Christiansen (who brought Mancini's remarks to my attention) has suggested in conversation that several painters in the wake of Caravaggio consciously avoided the posed or immobile appearance of his figures by using looser brushwork to convey movement and the play of light. This approach, which is implied, along with much else, by the critical term *colore*, went back to Titian and flourished before Caravaggio, with artists of such dissimilar inclinations as Barendsz and El Greco. But in the decades following Caravaggio's death in 1610 the use of a painterly manner became more closely linked with the notion of working directly "from life," as is seen in pictures by the French Caravaggesque painter Valentin de Boulogne (1591–1632), by Orazio Borgianni (see fig. 25) and other Italians, by Rubens, Jordaens, and Van Dyck (see figs. 22, 26), by Jusepe de Ribera in the 1630s, and by other masters whose careers coincided with that of Hals.

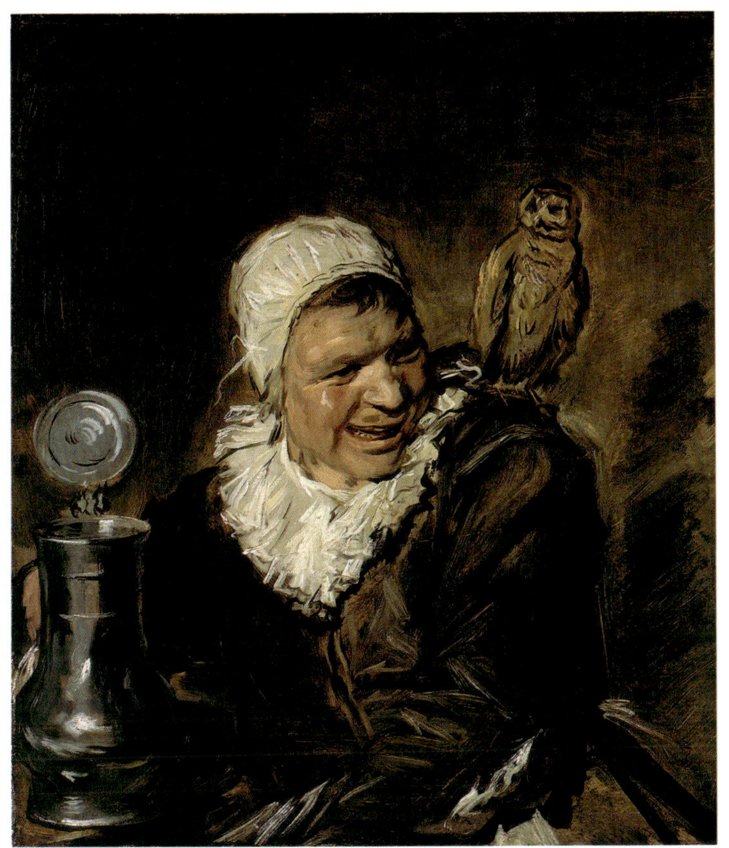

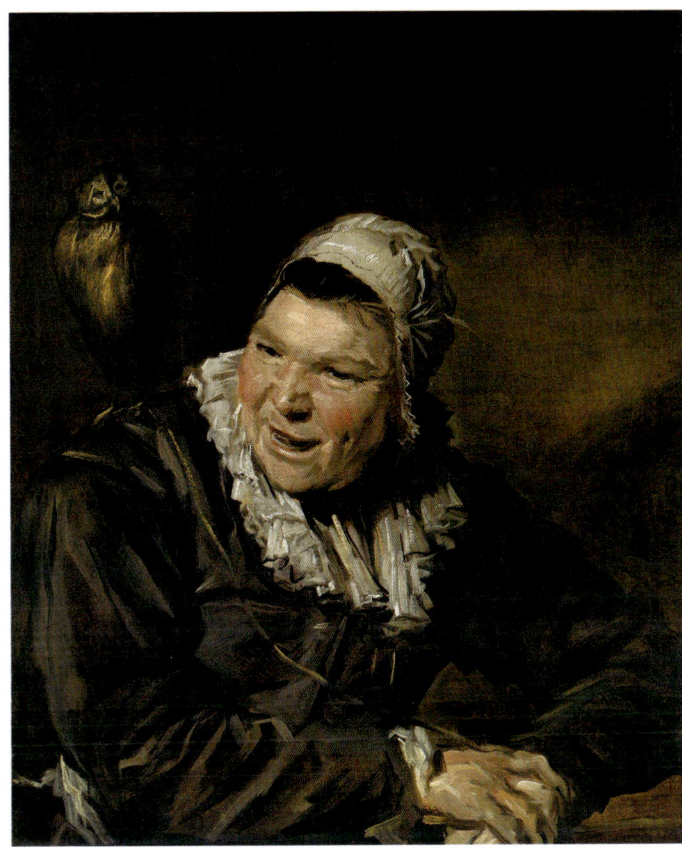

His example was certainly the most conspicuous in the northern Netherlands, and there can be little doubt that his particular style was largely his own creation. But its purpose would have been widely understood.

Vasari made another remark about Titian that is relevant to Hals, who would have considered it common sense. After describing how Titian's bold brushwork creates the impression of life when seen at the proper distance, Vasari observed that many masters have tried to imitate the technique with clumsy results. "And this happens because, although many believe that [Titian's late paintings] are done without effort, such is not the case . . . , for they are gone over again and again, and he returned to them with his colors so many times that much labor was involved. And this method, so used, is judicious, beautiful and astonishing, because it makes pictures appear alive and painted most artfully, but with the labor concealed."[38]

The same misunderstanding of the master's technique is obvious in pictures by Hals's immediate followers (as seen in figs. 27 and 28), in imitations and fakes dating from the nineteenth and twentieth centuries, and in Houbraken's remarks of 1718 to the effect that, with no underpainting or other preparation, Hals dashed off a portrait of Van Dyck. Variations on this theme date from the next 250 years, and often later.[39] According to J. D. Descamps (1753), Hals not only seized the first canvas to hand for his portrait of Van Dyck but "arranged the palette badly." Somewhat more sensibly, Joshua Reynolds, in a discourse to the Royal Academy in 1774, maintained that "Frank Halls" lacked "patience in finishing what he had so correctly planned." In the 1790s the Parisian art dealer J.-P.-B. Le Brun also regretted Hals's lack of finish, which in his view came from painting "so quickly . . . , [and] that which has been quickly executed is similarly regarded."[40] The presumption of rapid brushwork can be heard in gallery discussions of Hals to the present day; it is one of the many Romantic notions about painters (such impetuous spirits!) that still

27. Frans Hals. *Malle Babbe*, ca. 1633–35. Oil on canvas, 28 x 25¼ in. (78.5 x 66.2 cm). Gemäldegalerie, Staatliche Museen zu Berlin (801C). Malle Babbe (a name similar to Mad Meg) was a real person who was confined in the same charitable institution in Haarlem as Hals's mentally impaired son, Pieter. The owl was a common symbol of folly in the Netherlands.

28. Style of Frans Hals. *Malle Babbe*, probably ca. 1635–50. Oil on canvas, 29½ x 24 in. (74.9 x 61 cm). The Metropolitan Museum of Art, Purchase, 1871 (71.76). Although it was one of the proudest trophies of the "1871 Purchase" that formed the Museum's collection when it opened in 1872, this version of the Berlin picture (fig. 27) was rejected from Hals's oeuvre as early as 1883.

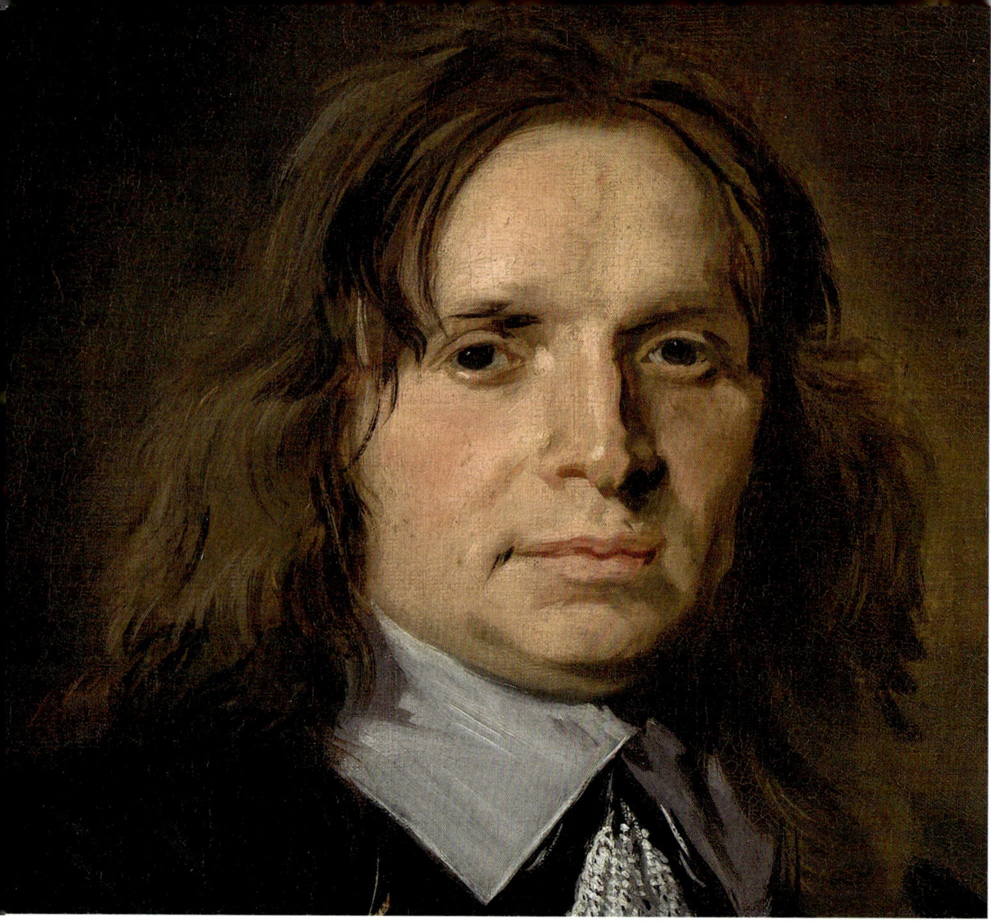

29. Frans Hals. *Portrait of a Man*, ca. 1650–55. Oil on canvas, 43½ x 34 in. (110.5 x 86.4 cm). The Metropolitan Museum of Art, Marquand Collection, Gift of Henry G. Marquand, 1890 (91.26.9). Hals used versions of this pose from about 1620 onward. The looped ribbons at the waist (called *tablier de galants*) and flouncing of the sleeves above tight cuffs were fashions imported from France.

30. Detail of fig. 29

survive. In *Dead Souls* (1842), Nikolai Gogol echoed a long tradition of art criticism (not going back to Vasari, however) when he warned the reader that his detailed picture of provincial society, and of his protagonist Chichikov, would require great patience to complete. "It is much easier to portray large-sized characters: just whirl your arm and fling paint on the canvas, dark scorching eyes, beetling brows, a furrow-creased forehead, a cloak, black or fiery scarlet, thrown over one shoulder—and the portrait is done."[41]

Nothing like this idea of impromptu painting is gained from reading a conservator's remarks on Hals, or from carefully looking at his pictures. From the former one learns that Hals probably purchased many of his canvases and panels already primed, usually with an oil-bound ground ranging in tone from off-white and light pink to an ocherous brown or cool gray.[42] Most of the ground layers in Hals's mature pictures are covered by the upper paint layers, but they are used in some works as a visible mid-tone in the background or in drapery, and may sometimes be seen through translucent areas of linen (collars and cuffs) and flesh. No drawings by Hals are known, although he may have used simple compositional sketches on occasion and then (as was normal in this period) discarded them. In any event, the actual painting began with a summary sketch of the figure or figures on the ground, using a brush to paint black or brownish lines. The large group portraits in Haarlem reveal revisions at various stages of the painting process, and this flexible approach was obviously foreseen by Hals whenever he sketched a face, figure, or other motif on a canvas.

The next phase of work, and the one least consistent with the image of Hals wielding his brush like Errol Flynn or Douglas Fairbanks engaged in Hollywood swordplay, consisted of laying in broad areas of colored "underpaints." Black clothing was usually painted on top of thin washes of brown or gray, which was selectively mixed in the studio. For example, the underpaint beneath the costume of *Portrait of a Man* (fig. 29) is a blend of lead white and carbon black, with a little yellow ocher and umber added. Flesh parts, by contrast, would be underpainted in white (lead white mixed with chalk beneath the bare hand of *Paulus Verschuur*; see fig. 31) or, more commonly, a pinkish or reddish tone. On these areas of what was called "dead coloring" in Hals's day, he would sometimes paint light lines to clarify the position of an arm or other motif, probably because the underpainting had partly obscured the first sketch on the priming.

What is now visible, for the most part, in a painting by Hals came in the fourth stage, which was the most complex—really several campaigns of *opmaecken*, or "working up." Here Hals would have used more than one brush in a session of painting, often bringing along the background and part of the figure at nearly the same time. In general, costumes were finished before heads and hands, but many adjustments could

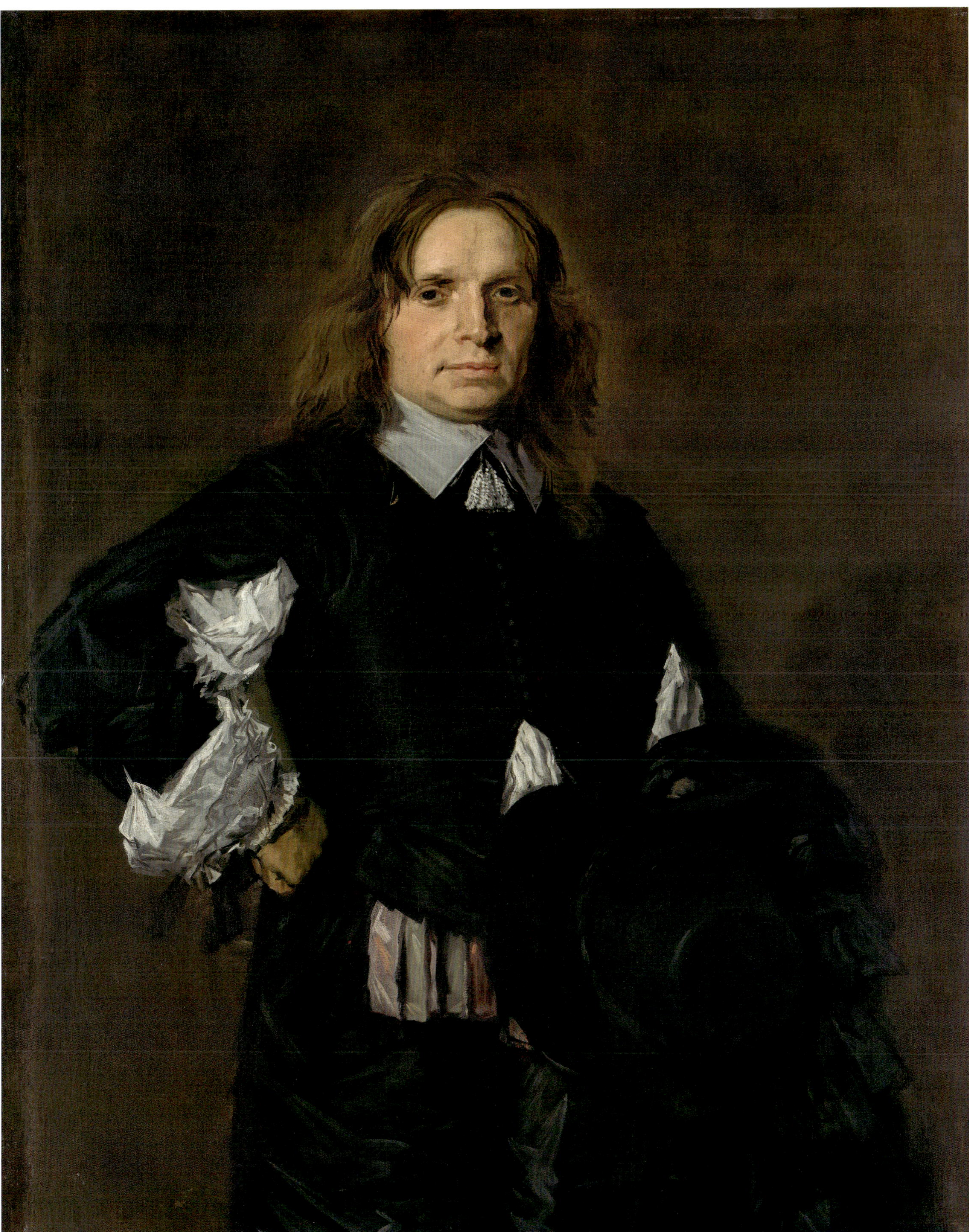

31. Frans Hals. *Paulus Verschuur*, 1643. Oil on canvas, 46¾ x 37 in. (118.7 x 94 cm). The Metropolitan Museum of Art, Gift of Archer M. Huntington, in memory of his father, Collis Potter Huntington, 1926 (26.101.11). Verschuur, a wealthy merchant of Rotterdam, is seen here at the age of thirty-seven. At the time he served on the Rotterdam city council, and he went on to hold several high offices locally and in the national government.

still be made, for instance by interrupting and blurring contour lines for atmospheric effect or by making wisps of hair blend into the background or cascade onto a collar (see fig. 30). Hair was often painted while the background was still wet, just as many of the more translucent highlights on the costumes were blended into the overall tones. (Van Gogh observed that "Frans Hals must have had twenty-seven blacks.")[43] A portrait was almost finished when Hals colored the lips and touched up the eyes, but a fair amount of fussing with contours, shadows, and highlights might have continued on the same or another day. One part of the process that is missing from Houbraken's story of a Van Dyck portrait painted by Hals is the artist's constant stepping back to see how a passage or the whole looked from a distance. Another missing detail is where Van Dyck found a room for a few nights.

Accomplished artists of Hals's own century and the next two—one thinks of admirers such as Gustave Courbet, Édouard Manet, John Singer Sargent, and William Merritt Chase—surely understood just by looking at his paintings that he devoted a lot of care to preparing and finishing his work. But quite as Courbet, in his "copy" after Hals's *Malle Babbe* (fig. 27), emphasized the qualities that most attracted him, artist-writers such as Houbraken and Reynolds faulted Hals's lack of finish because finish is what they and connoisseurs of their time preferred.[44] (The Paris dealer Le Brun's business depended extensively on pictures by "fine painters" such as Gerrit Dou and Gabriël Metsu.) There can be little doubt that Houbraken knew that his own story about Hals's rapid execution was implausible on technical grounds. In his critique of Rembrandt, about whom Houbraken understood a great deal through his teacher Van Hoogstraten, the same sort of rhetorical license is evident. According to Houbraken, Rembrandt carefully carried out and completed many pictures, especially in his early years, but later on the master lost patience, was easily distracted, and became a capricious sort. And yet Houbraken was well aware that such shifts in style were really a matter of taste, not character. The best of Rembrandt's pupils (Govert Flinck, Nicolaes Maes, et al.), he tells us, adopted a brighter and more finished manner as soon as they saw the light (shed by Van Dyck and other fashionable portraitists).[45]

Judging the question for oneself in front of paintings by Hals is a revealing and rewarding exercise. In faces like those of Duyst van Voorhout (fig. 5) and the sitter in *Portrait of a Man* (figs. 29, 30), fluid highlights and blunt shadows, all with visible strokes, suggest daylight playing over moist and pliant skin. But what is more remarkable is that the same strokes, especially when seen at a normal viewing distance, sculpt the features emphatically; the volume and structure of a head is made clear whether the facial features are soft and puffy (as in fig. 5) or firm and angular (as in fig. 31). Brushstrokes that very much resemble each other when seen close up, like the dark strokes in *Portrait of a Man* that sketch the eyebrows, carve out the bridge of the nose, and tick off deep indentations at the corners of the mouth (see fig. 30), serve different descriptive functions when the viewer steps back. Hals often painted a thick black line along one side of the jaw and under the chin, which seems to sit on the surface when studied closely (almost as if it were a later addition) but at a distance reads as deep shadow, projecting the face forward.

All this Hals achieved while maintaining a consistent light source, which is far more complicated than it might at first appear. The viewer who is diverted by the electric linen, fancy ribbons, and tousled hair in *Portrait of a Man* (fig. 29) might overlook how the right side of the jacket is muted compared with the left, how the

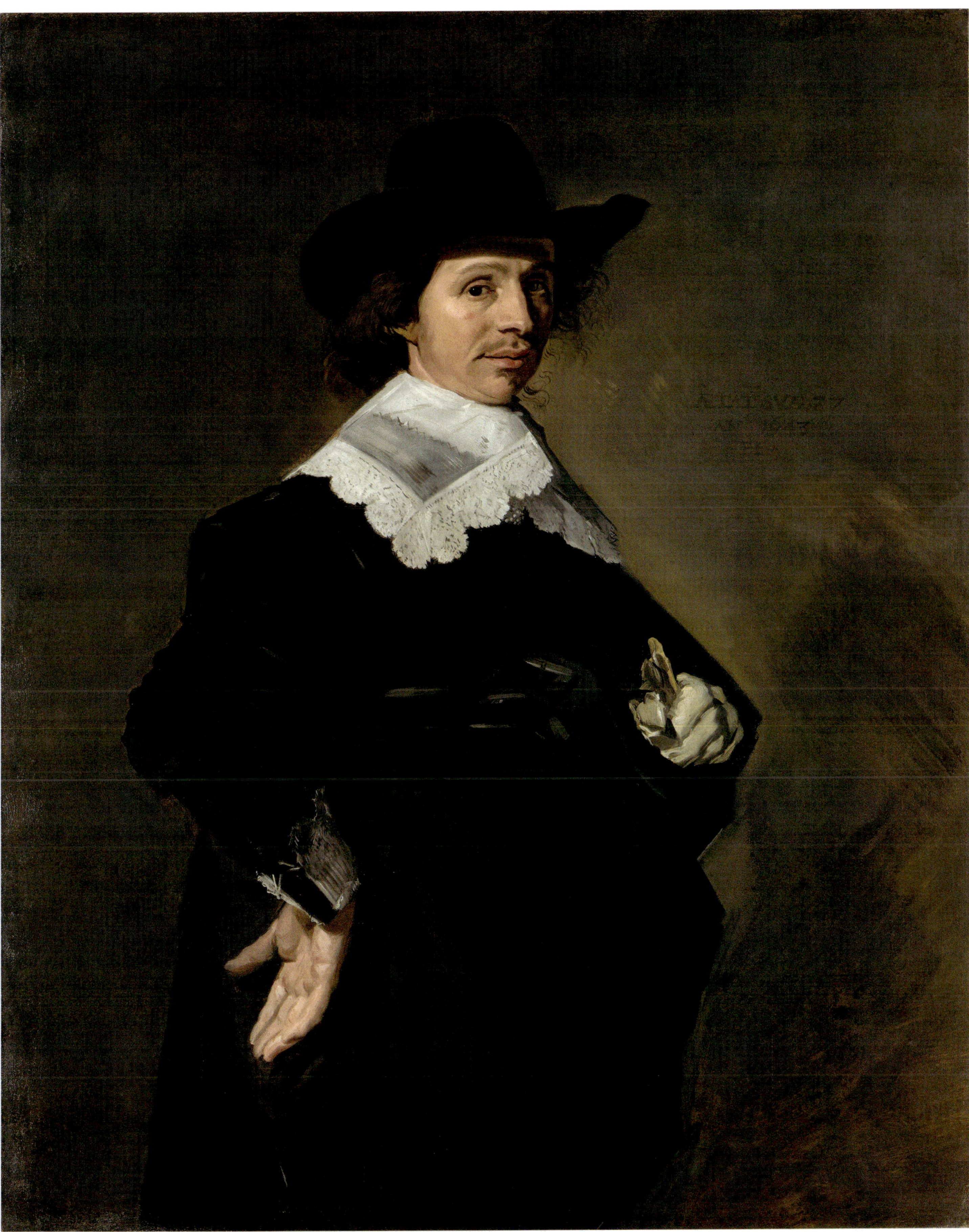

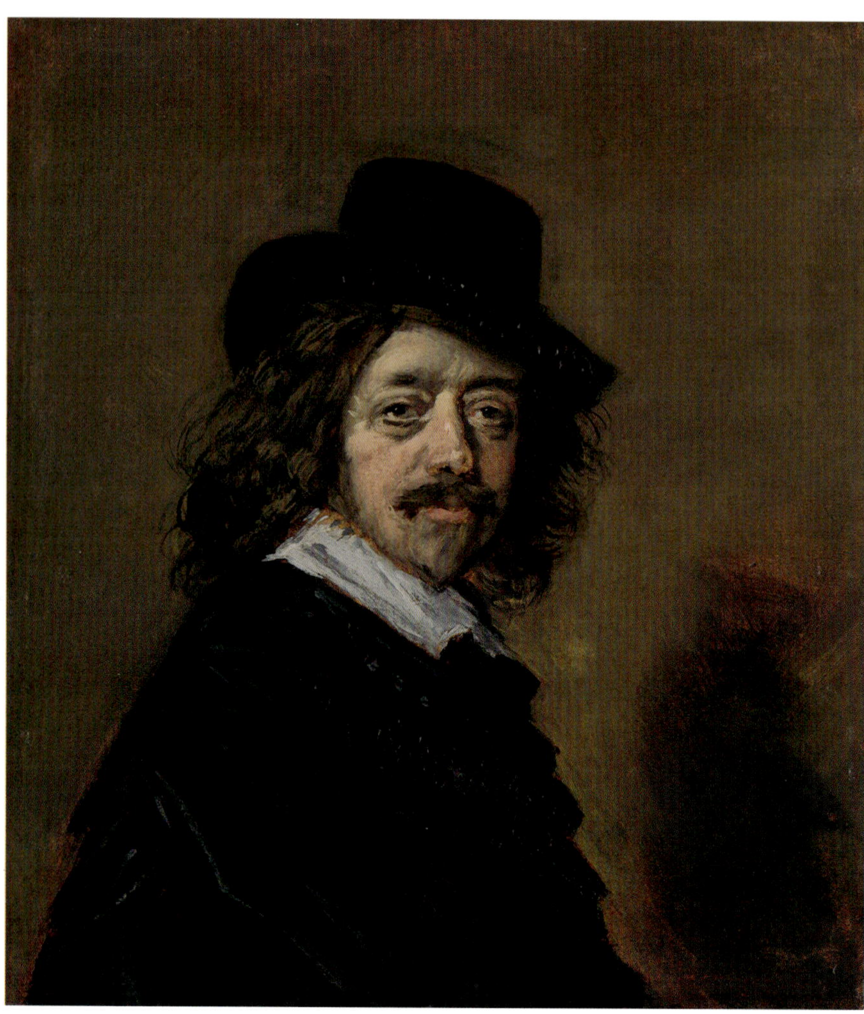

32. Copy after Frans Hals. *Frans Hals*, probably 1650s. Oil on wood, 12⅞ x 11 in. (32.7 x 27.9 cm). The Metropolitan Museum of Art, The Friedsam Collection, Bequest of Michael Friedsam, 1931 (32.100.8). There are a few such copies after a lost self-portrait by Hals, the best being in the Indianapolis Museum of Art.

wedge of white sleeve to the right is toned down with gray, or how differently the sides of the face are colored and modeled. In the portrait of Paulus Verschuur (fig. 31), so much of the spatial effect in the foreground depends on the black slashes of shadow to the right of the near arm and hand: covering them turns the wrapped mantle into an apron and the arm held akimbo into a limp appendage. Not only his expression and pose but also the fall of light and its evocation of form and space tell the viewer that Verschuur, although less outgoing than the unidentified gentleman in *Portrait of a Man*, was a person of substance.

These qualities of form, space, independent light, and atmosphere, and the suggestion of various textures (which are not, however, worn on the sleeve, as in pictures by some Dutch artists), were still completely in evidence when Hals painted a head two or three inches high, as in the portrait of Petrus Scriverius (fig. 37). Even Houbraken could not concoct a tale about painting this panel quickly: Hals would have been bent over the image for many hours, lightly touching the surface with the tip of a fine brush. The face and bust make for a useful comparison with a slightly larger portrait, the Museum's period copy of a lost self-portrait (fig. 32). Here the painter was attempting to match a model by Hals—stroke for stroke, as it were—and yet the result is incoherent, a flat surface with some shapes shoved together, and prosaic summaries of where Hals had placed a body in space and put a hat on the head. Of course, the copyist's shortcoming was a question not just of talent but also of the psychological difference between looking at a two-dimensional plane (Hals's original picture or another copy of it) and the perception of actual forms in three-dimensional space. The same gulf between a compelling image and brushwork smeared onto canvas or wood is frequently found when comparing works by Rembrandt and his lesser followers. The latter emulate the slashes, jabs, and pasty highlights that they saw in their master's example, but the viewer cannot see through the surface and find the character that once stood before the painter or at least appeared in his mind.

What Hals saw in his sitters, or thought about his subjects, was touched upon in Joshua Reynolds's remarks to the Royal Academy. Hals's brushwork (to which Reynolds preferred Van Dyck's late, smooth manner) did not, from an academic perspective, follow to completion what the artist "had so correctly planned." In the same passage Reynolds admired in Hals's portraits "the composition of a face, the features well put together, as the painters express it; from whence proceeds that strong-marked character of individual nature, which is so remarkable in

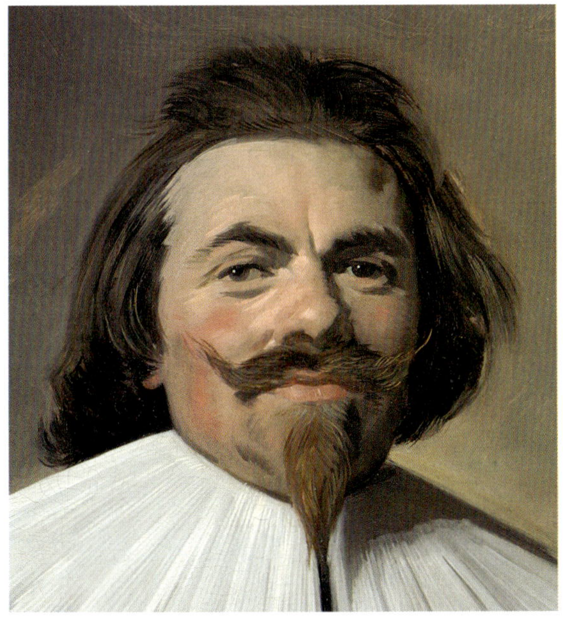

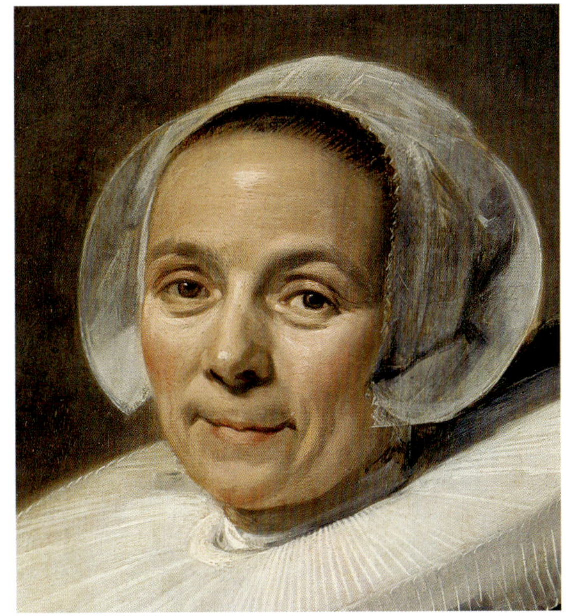

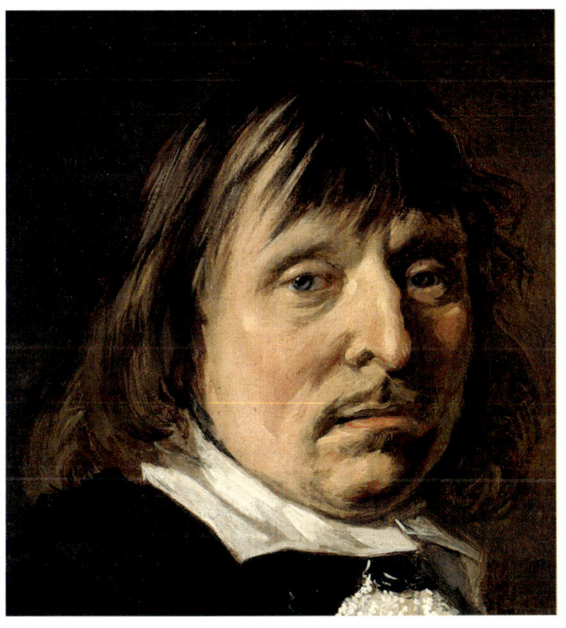

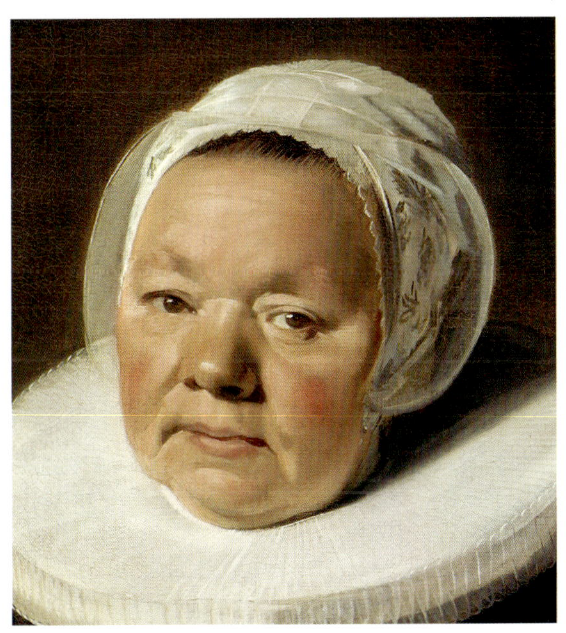

33. Details of faces in portraits by Frans Hals. Top left: *Tieleman Roosterman*, 1634. Oil on canvas, 46⅛ x 34¼ in. (117 x 87 cm). The Cleveland Museum of Art, Leonard C. Hanna, Jr. Fund (1999.173). Top right: *Portrait of a Woman*, 1638. Oil on canvas, 37 x 28 in. (94 x 71 cm). Städel Museum, Frankfurt am Main (5739). Bottom left: *Tyman Oosdorp*, 1656. Oil on canvas, 32¼ x 29 in. (82 x 73.5 cm). Gemäldegalerie, Staatliche Museen zu Berlin (801H). Bottom right: *Portrait of a Woman*, 1635. Oil on canvas, 45⅞ x 36¾ in. (116.5 cm x 93.4 cm). The Frick Collection, New York, Henry Clay Frick Bequest (1910.1.72)

his portraits, and is not found in an equal degree in any other painter."

This is quite a compliment, considering that it comes from a great admirer of Rubens and Rembrandt. And it encourages the modern viewer to step back from the picture surface not only to see the physical effect of Hals's portraits, their immediacy and animation, but also to survey his gift for analyzing—or, at least, projecting—individual character (see fig. 33). This ability is not equally evident in every work. Many of Hals's portraits suggest friendliness, preoccupation, or reserve, without giving away much about the person. The emphasis placed in our time on personal thoughts and feelings was barely beginning in the seventeenth century, with exceptional authors such as Shakespeare and John Donne. Hals's wonderful portraits of married couples and families, like the large group portrait in the Museo Thyssen-Bornemisza, Madrid (fig. 34), convey a strong sense of individuality but are essentially about the institution of marriage. Similarly, many of Hals's sitters wanted to be portrayed as representatives of a certain type or class. It is precisely in this context

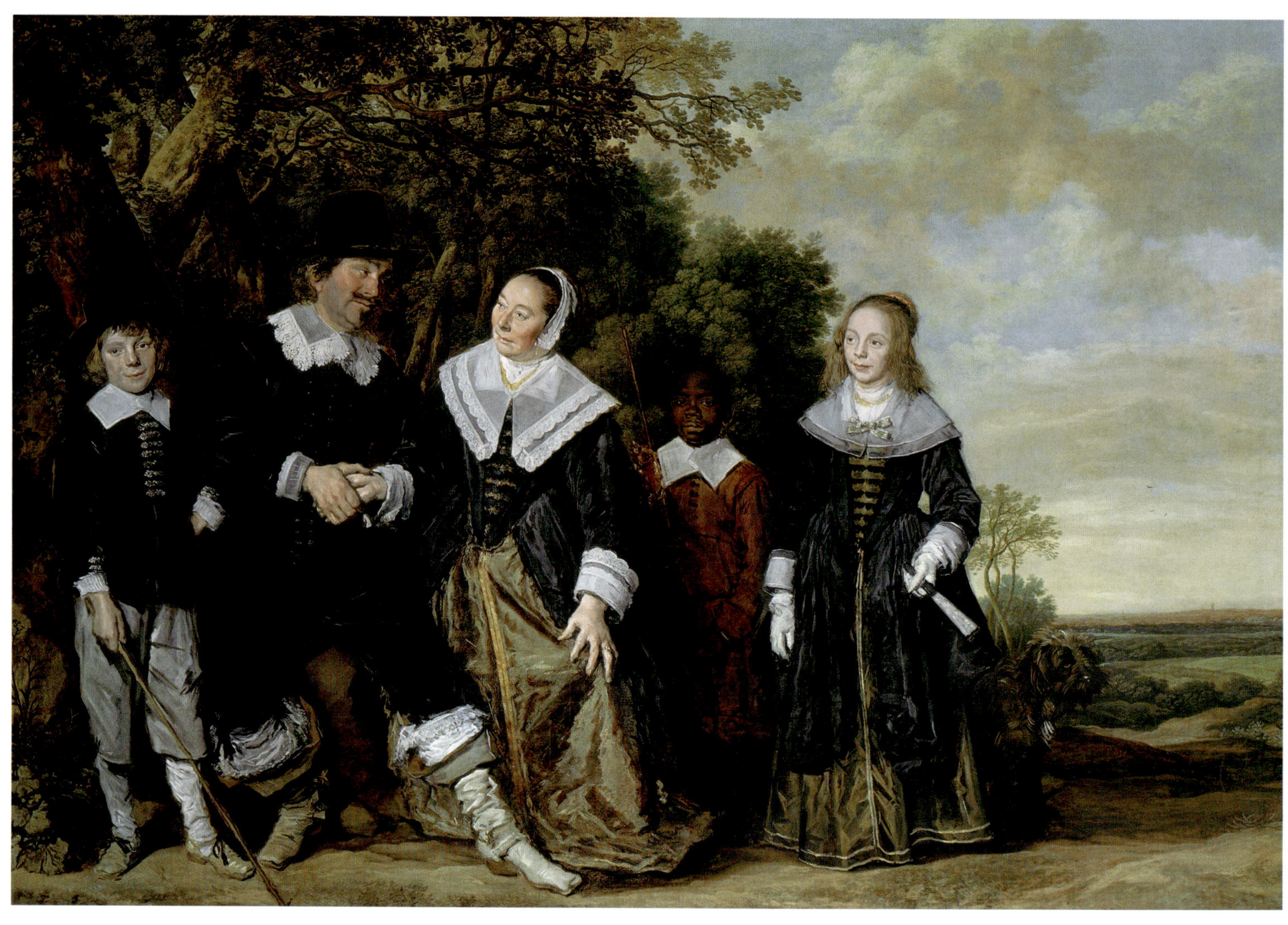

34. Frans Hals. *Family Group in a Landscape*, ca. 1648. Oil on canvas, 79½ x 112 in. (202 x 285 cm). Museo Thyssen-Bornemisza, Madrid (179 [1934.8]). Although the clasped hands, a symbol of marriage, derive from emblem books and marriage medals, the figures' poses and expressions are remarkable for their immediacy. The landscape to the right is most likely by Hals's Haarlem colleague Pieter de Molijn (1595–1661).

of strong social conventions that Hals's frequently compelling sense of individual character is so remarkable. There is hardly anything like it in the oeuvre of his very gifted competitor in Haarlem, Johannes Verspronck (see fig. 35), or in any contemporary artist except for Rembrandt. This is actually made clear in one gallery of The Metropolitan Museum of Art, where two or three large portraits by Hals usually hang in the same room as six or seven by Rembrandt. The occasional intrusion of a portrait by some other Dutch specialist most frequently gives the impression of an odd man out. But to express it this way is to stand history on its head: Hals and Rembrandt produced exceptional portraits, in a field of Dutch art which, more than any other, was notable for its conformity.

Here Hals had the advantage of working in Haarlem, where some of his upper-middle-class patrons (including members of the civic guard companies) were open to novel and generally more dramatic ideas in portraiture. In the period 1600–1650 (and also later, in the case of Amsterdam) the neighboring cities of northern Holland, Haarlem and Amsterdam, were growing as commercial centers, and new money played a larger role in the art market than in the other major centers of the United Provinces. Hals in the 1620s and Rembrandt after moving from Leiden to Amsterdam in about 1632 introduced new forms of animation and expression into portraiture that would not have been expected in the court city of The Hague, where the staid conventions that are typified by the work of Michiel van Miereveld (1567–1641) were preferred. The court style of portraiture (which had strong roots in the dour tradition of Spain) prevailed also in The Hague's satellite city, Delft (where the prince's portraitist, Van Miereveld, actually lived), in the university city of Leiden (where most of the Dutch gentry were educated), and even in Utrecht, where Paulus Moreelse (1571–1638) followed Van Miereveld's example and the court favorite Van Honthorst was at his least creative in the realm of portraiture. There were exceptions on the Dutch map of taste, to be sure: in the same year as Hals did, 1616, The Hague's reliably bland portraitist Jan van Ravesteyn (ca. 1572–1657) came up with an inventive solution to the problem of portraying a large group in his *Officers and Guardsmen of the Orange Company of The Hague on the Steps of the Town Hall* (Haags Historisch Museum, The Hague). But Hals never would have become such an innovative portrait or genre painter had he pursued a career in another part of the northern Netherlands.[46]

The Museum's *Portrait of a Bearded Man*, dated 1625 (fig. 36), is one of several comparatively early works in which Hals presented the sitter in a manner that would have been unexpected elsewhere in the Dutch Republic. A painted oval frame defines the picture surface and places the figure emphatically behind it, responding to the viewer with a literally "heartfelt" gesture of sincerity. Hals had already used the same framing device in a slightly more radical way about a decade earlier, in his *Portrait of a Man Holding a Medallion* (Brooklyn Museum, New York). In that canvas of nearly the same size, the sitter's hand, holding a miniature portrait of a woman, projects through the oval frame, and his torso recedes at a stronger angle to the picture plane. Oval frames had been employed since the 1570s in portrait prints by Goltzius and his contemporaries, and in some examples the figure extends beyond the frame.[47] The first Dutch artist known to have used the device in a painting of normal size (meant to hang on a wall) was not Hals but a printmaker in Goltzius's circle, Gerrit Pietersz (1566–before ca. 1612), in a portrait dated 1606 of his brother, the composer Jan Pietersz Sweelinck (Gemeentemuseum, The Hague). As Slive has observed, only portraits that are near lifesize make a figure reaching through a frame look illusionistic.[48]

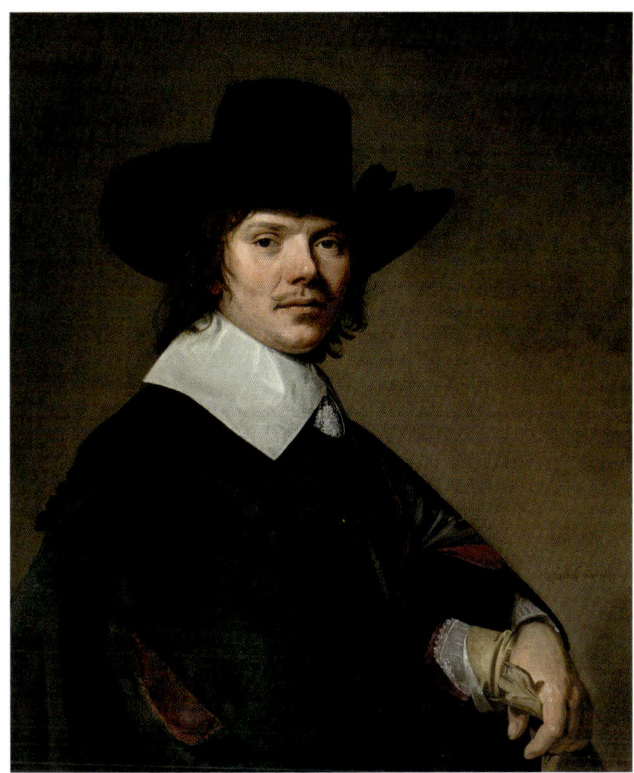

35. Johannes Verspronck (Dutch, Haarlem, ca. 1601/3–1662 Haarlem). *Portrait of a Man*, 1645. Oil on canvas, 31¼ x 25¼ in. (79.4 x 64.1 cm). The Metropolitan Museum of Art, Bequest of Susan P. Colgate, in memory of her husband, Romulus R. Colgate, 1936 (36.162.1). Verspronck was Catholic, and many of his sitters were prominent Catholics in Haarlem, although Calvinist patrons often sat for the painter as well. Unlike Hals, he employed a restricted range of compositional patterns and careful underdrawings, which the paint layers closely follow.

Hals intensified the trompe-l'oeil effect in the portrait of 1625 by strongly modeling the figure with light and shadow (note the range of shadows cast to the right of the man's nose and cheek and on the ruff and wall), by blurring contours, and by streaking different kinds of highlights throughout the costume and on the hand and face. The overall impression of "life itself" would have been enhanced by the sort of light that was available in a seventeenth-century interior, which (whether from an oil lamp, candles, or windows) would have been much less steady and bright than modern museum lighting. And, of course, there was no such thing as a "moving image" in Hals's day, but there were, in his case, pictures "imbued with such force and vitality

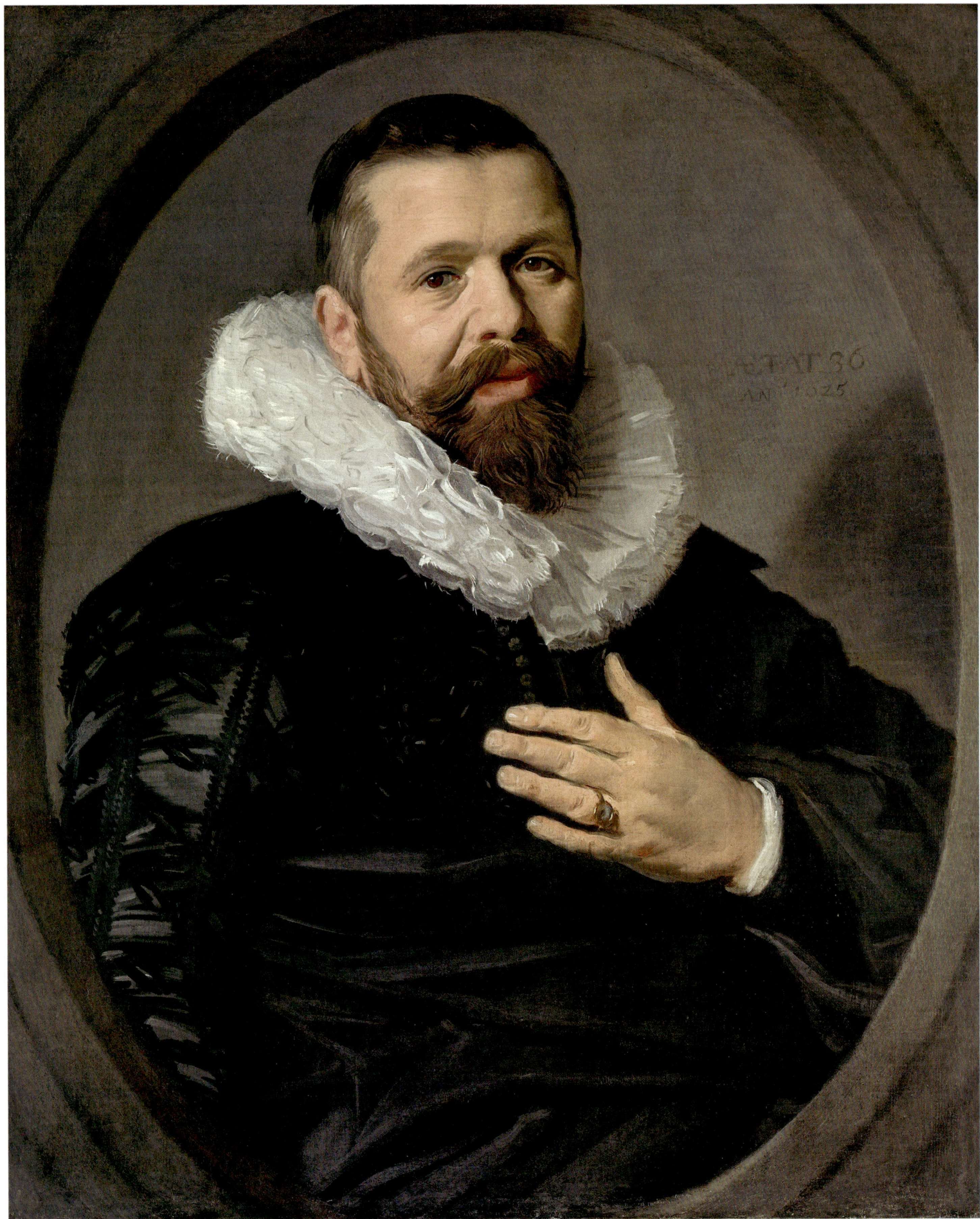

that he seems to defy nature herself with his brush," and portraits painted so that "they seem to live and breathe."

These words were written by one of Hals's own portrait subjects, Theodore Schrevelius, in his history of Haarlem, published in Latin and Dutch in 1647 and 1648, respectively.[49] Hals's small oval portrait of Schrevelius (Frans Hals Museum, Haarlem), one of three Hals portraits on copper, is dated 1617 and served as the model for Jacob Matham's engraving of the following year.[50] The print bears an inscription by another Latin scholar, Petrus Scriverius (1576–1660), whose small portrait by Hals and the pendant portrait of Scriverius's wife, Anna van der Aar (figs. 37, 38), are each signed in monogram and dated 1626. The pair of panels was purchased in Paris by the celebrated collectors of Impressionist pictures Henry and Louisine Havemeyer in 1889 and left to the Museum in 1929 as part of the extraordinary Havemeyer Bequest.[51]

Here again Hals presented the figures within fictive frames. The male sitter's hand rests on the bottom of the oval molding and holds a pair of gloves (the attribute of a gentleman) in front of it. His portrait alone was reproduced in an engraving, also of 1626, by the Haarlem artist Jan van de Velde II (fig. 39). In the print the spatial effect of the frame, hand, and gloves is enhanced, so that the portrait seems to project like a relief above the base bearing an "anonymous" (Scriverian) inscription in Latin: "Here you see the face of him who, shunning public office, makes the Muses his own at personal expense," and so on.

Scriverius spent most of his time as an independent scholar, publishing commentaries on classical authors as well as histories of the Netherlands and particular provinces. At the age of seventeen he went from Haarlem's flourishing Latin School to the University of Leiden, and six years later, in 1599, he married Anna, daughter of Willem Govertsz van der Aar, a prominent textile merchant in Leiden. Willem's brother Jan Govertsz van der Aar was one of the greatest patrons of the arts in Haarlem, the subject of an outstanding portrait by Goltzius (1603; Museum Boijmans Van Beuningen, Rotterdam) and a supporter of all the leading Mannerist artists in the city.[52] Although Scriverius lived with his in-laws in the center of Leiden, he maintained close contacts with Haarlem, to which canal boats departed ten times a day. His parents were living in Haarlem when they both died in 1626, and Scriverius collaborated on Samuel Ampzing's ambitious book about the city, *Beschryvinge ende lof der stad Haerlem in Holland* (Description and Praise of the City of Haarlem in Holland), which was published there in 1628. Hals's work was mentioned in print for the first time in the *Description and Praise*, as part of Ampzing's poetic tribute to Haarlem artists: "How dashingly Frans paints people from life!" Ampzing made special mention of the Calivermen civic guard portrait dating from the previous year (fig. 16).[53]

Hals's superb portrait of Ampzing (fig. 40), on copper, was painted in 1630 and shows him holding what must be the volume of 1628. Many of its illustrations were engraved by Jan van de Velde II, who upon Ampzing's death in 1632 made a print after Hals's portrait. Below the image a Latin poem, signed *P.S.*, describes how the author's memory may be traced especially in the scars he inflicted on the "Ausonian Bishop" (meaning Catholic prelates, Ausonia being a name the ancient Greek and Latin poets used for Italy) and "the Spaniard's Brow."[54]

For his own portrait (fig. 37), Scriverius probably turned to Hals in Haarlem rather than a Leiden specialist like David Bailly (1584–1657) because he admired the Schrevelius portrait and the engraving after it. Portrait prints of scholars were sent to colleagues and institutions throughout Europe, usually as gifts from the subjects themselves. One year before Hals painted

36. Frans Hals. *Portrait of a Bearded Man with a Ruff*, 1625. Oil on canvas, 30 x 25 in. (76.2 x 63.5 cm). The Metropolitan Museum of Art, The Jules Bache Collection, 1949 (49.7.34). In the Netherlands in the seventeenth century expensive but conservative attire (compare fig. 1) was restrained in color but rich in fabric combinations and details, which Hals's highlights emphasize. The contrast between the bright and shadowy sides of the ruff is typical of Hals, spatially effective, and dazzling in technique.

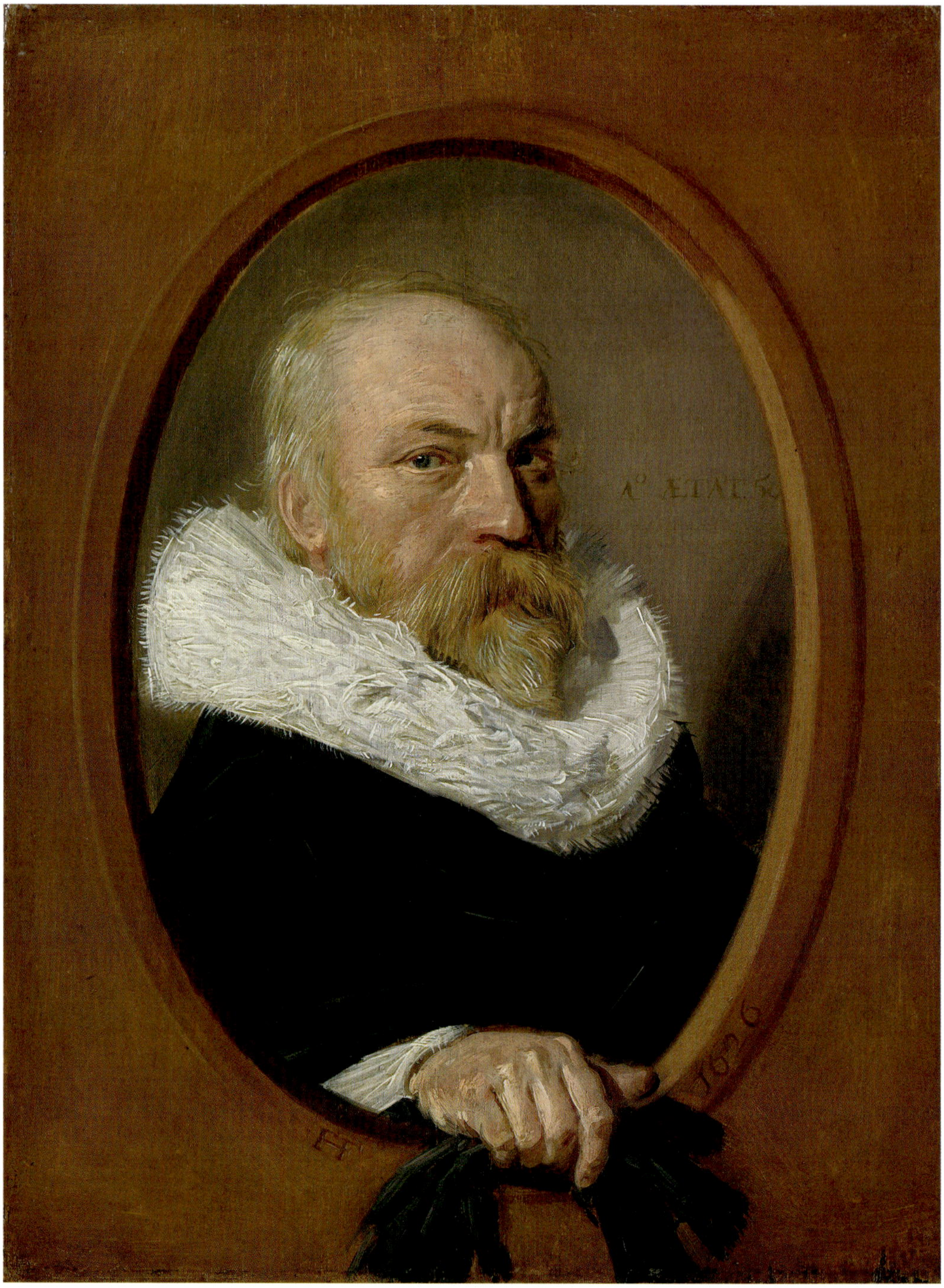

37. Frans Hals. *Petrus Scriverius*, 1626. Oil on wood, 8¾ x 6½ in. (22.2 x 16.5 cm). The Metropolitan Museum of Art, H. O. Havemeyer Collection, Bequest of Mrs. H. O. Havemeyer, 1929 (29.100.8). Scriverius was a highly regarded Latin scholar and historian of the Dutch provinces. The small scale of this portrait facilitated its reproduction as an engraving (see fig. 39).

39. Jan van de Velde II (Dutch, Rotterdam or Delft ca. 1593–1641 Enkhuizen) after Frans Hals. *Petrus Scriverius*, 1626. Engraving, 10½ x 6⅛ in. (26.6 x 15.5 cm). The Metropolitan Museum of Art, Gift of Carl J. Ulmann, 1924 (24.57.27). Engraved portraits of scholars like this one were often commissioned by the sitters and sent to colleagues and institutions throughout Europe.

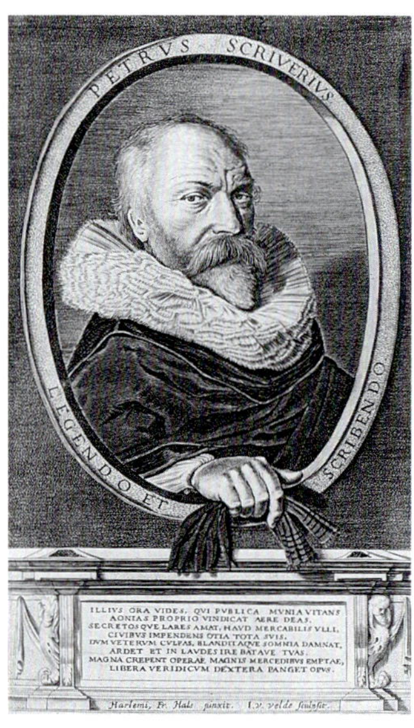

the Havemeyer panels, Schrevelius moved to Leiden, as the new rector of the Latin School. His portrait by Hals came with him, for in 1628 he showed it to the visiting diarist and art lover Aernout van Buchell (Buchelius), to whom he also gave an impression of Van de Velde's portrait, after Hals, of Scriverius (fig. 39). In both cases it is clear that the small painted portrait of a scholar was made as a keepsake and as a model for an engraving—at once a personal memento and a claim to international fame.

It cannot be claimed on the basis of his academic portraits that Hals moved in intellectual rather than inebriated circles, but they do underscore the point, made by scholars such as Biesboer, that the artist had a quite respectable clientele. Even the types of pictures that inspired Houbraken's defamatory account make a different impression when one learns of their literary

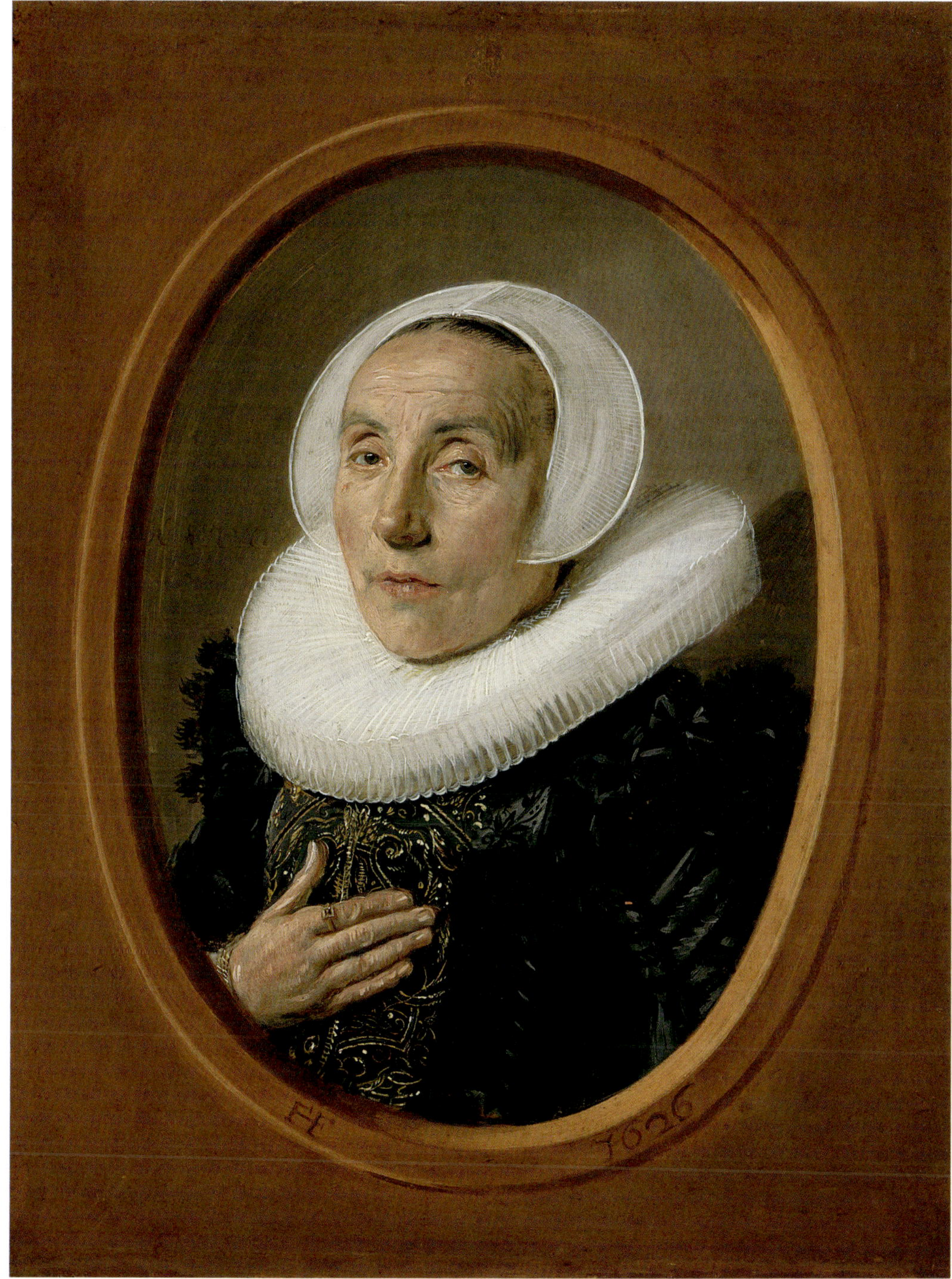

38. Frans Hals. *Anna van der Aar*, 1626. Oil on wood, 8¾ x 6½ in. (22.2 x 16.5 cm). The Metropolitan Museum of Art, H. O. Havemeyer Collection, Bequest of Mrs. H. O. Havemeyer, 1929 (29.100.9). This panel was painted as a pendant to the portrait of the sitter's husband but was not likewise engraved. Although they were residents of Leiden, the scholar and his spouse were well connected with artistic and literary circles in Haarlem.

parallels, such as Scriverius's attack on the *rederijkers* in 1616 (see figs. 7, 14), his tract against tobacco of 1628 (see fig. 24), and the emblem books and plays that were readily available in Haarlem. Some of Hals's most distinguished sitters, such as Jacob Olycan and his wife, Aletta Hanemans (their pendant portraits, of 1625, are in the Mauritshuis, The Hague), brought him many other commissions—at least eighteen portraits of members of the Olycan family, not counting Jacob's inclusion (as lieutenant) in the center of Hals's group portrait of the officers of the Saint George Civic Guard of about 1627 and his son-in-law Johan Schatter's appearance in the Calivermen civic guard picture of that year (fig. 16) and the same company's portrait of 1633.[55]

Family connections occasionally led Hals to clients in other cities, as in the case of Paulus Verschuur (fig. 31), a wealthy textile merchant of Rotterdam whose sister

40. Frans Hals. *Samuel Ampzing*, 1630. Oil on copper, 6⅜ x 4⅞ in. (16.2 x 12.3 cm). Private collection. Ampzing was a Haarlem historian, poet, and clergyman. His *Beschryvinge ende lof der stad Haerlem in Holland* (Description and Praise of the City of Haarlem in Holland) of 1628 celebrates Hals's portraits for the first time in print.

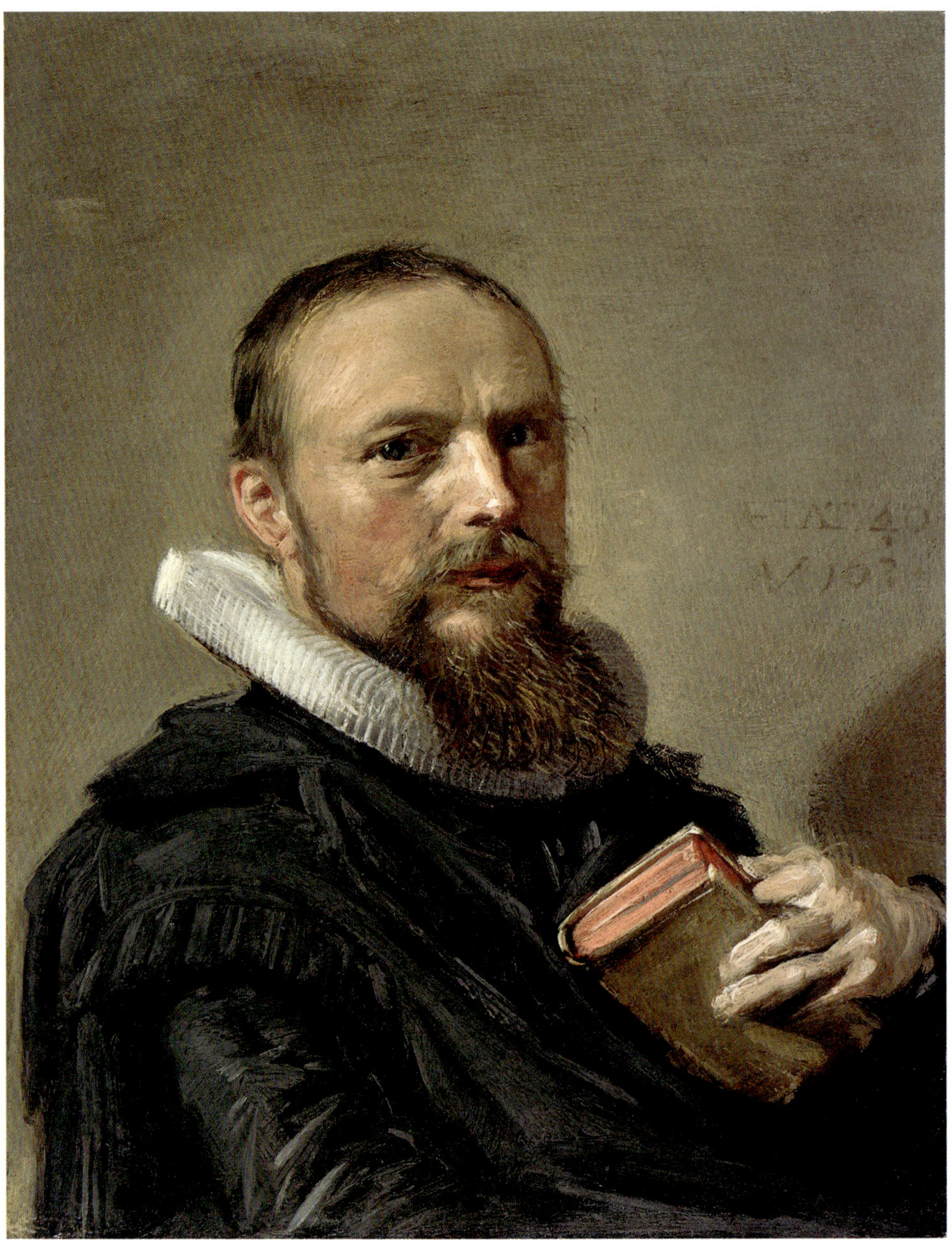

was married to a Haarlem Mennonite in the same business. Hals's one great project out of town, however, the magnificent civic guard picture known by the misleading title *The Meagre Company* (Rijksmuseum, Amsterdam), appears to have come to him in 1633 because of his recent successes with this type of public portraiture.[56] As it happens, work on the fourteen-foot-wide canvas (with less preparation than usual) progressed at rare intervals in Amsterdam, and in 1636 a series of angry exchanges led to the right half of the picture being reassigned to the gifted Amsterdam genre painter Pieter Codde (1599–1678).[57] He did an excellent job of harmonizing his manner of execution with that of Hals, but when Van Gogh saw the painting in 1885 he could not tear himself away from the most Halsian figure in the painting: the standard bearer to the far left, which Van Gogh described to his brother Theo as an astonishing ensemble of vivid colors that somehow formed a rhapsody in pearl gray.[58]

Van Gogh could not have seen *The Meagre Company* before 1885, the year in which the city of Amsterdam first lent the canvas to the Rijksmuseum. Like other civic guard companies, the Voetboogdoelen (Crossbow Civic Guard House) for which

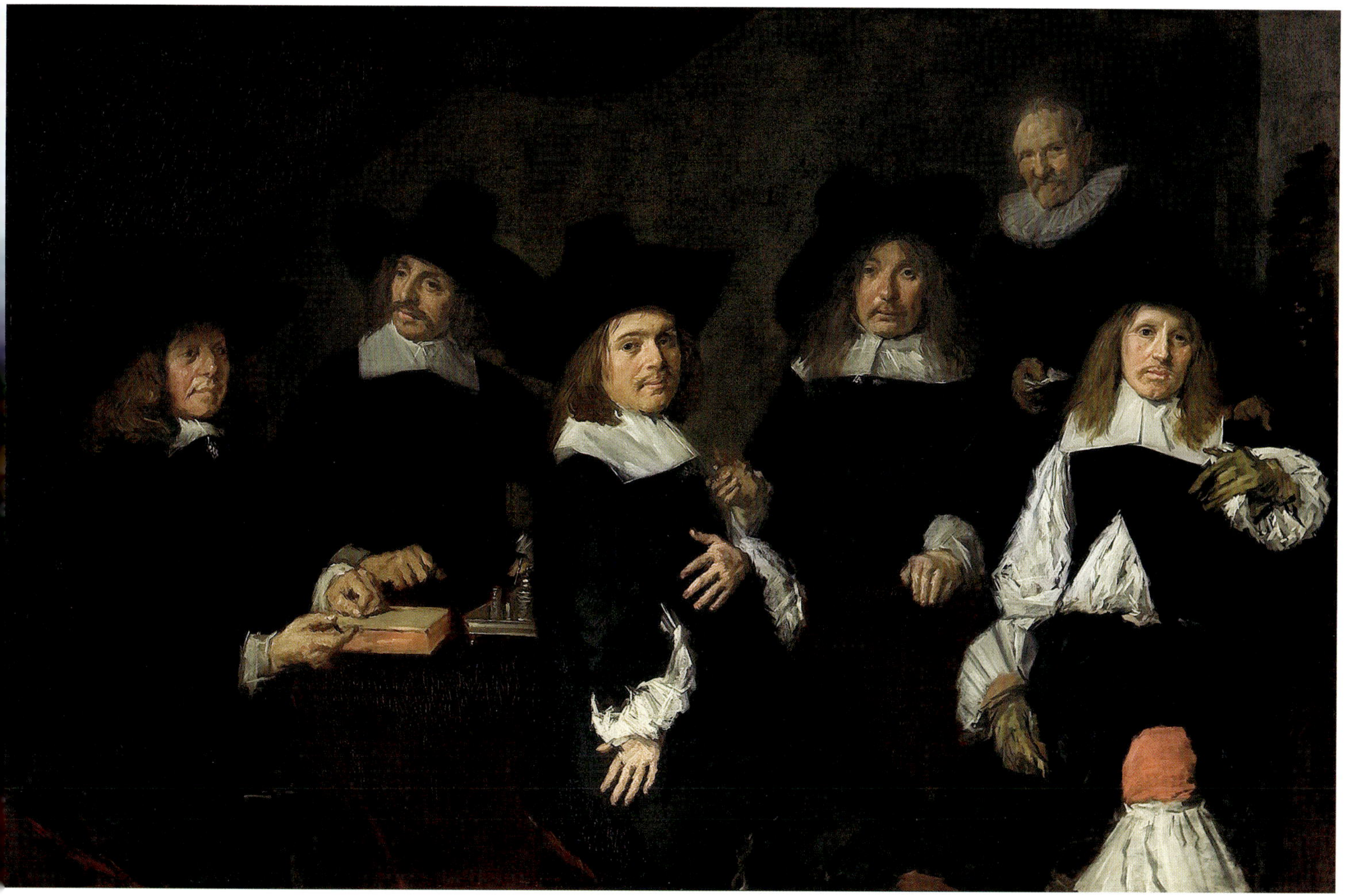

Hals painted the canvas was essentially a social club, and an anachronism even before Dutch independence was recognized in 1648. The building was rented to business organizations from 1674 onward and was destroyed in 1816. In Haarlem as well as in Amsterdam the great civic guard portraits (including Rembrandt's *Night Watch*) became city property and were placed on loan to their local museums. The Haarlem Municipal Museum (later renamed the Frans Hals Museum) opened in the Town Hall in 1862, allowing visiting painters—among them Monet in 1871 and Manet the next year—to comprehend the full extent of Hals's work for the first time.[59] This included the last group portraits, of the male and female regents of the Old Men's Almshouse (fig. 41), which Hals painted in about 1664 when he was about eighty-two years old.[60] Houbraken-like legends have it that Hals himself was an inmate of the Almshouse (the building that became the city's art museum in 1913) and that he painted the fourth regent from the left with a (fashionably) slanted hat and bleary look, once again indicating a boozer, because of some desire for revenge. Hals was indeed needy in his old age and received some subsidies and annuities from the city. The commission for the late group portraits may have been bestowed as a kindness as well as an honor. In any event, Hals lived and worked independently until his death in late August 1666. He was buried in Haarlem's Great Church, Saint Bavo's, on September 1 of that year.

The Metropolitan Museum of Art owes its eleven autograph works by Hals to great collectors of the Gilded Age. Except for Jules Bache's purchases of 1926 (fig. 36) and 1928 (fig. 5), all of the paintings were

41. Frans Hals. *Regents of the Old Men's Almshouse*, ca. 1664. Oil on canvas, 67⅞ x 100¾ in. (172.5 x 256 cm). Frans Hals Museum, Haarlem (os I-115). This canvas and its better preserved pendant, *Regentesses of the Old Men's Almshouse*, also in the Frans Hals Museum, are remarkable for their suggestions of character and broad brushwork. The pictures were meant to be seen at a considerably greater distance than they generally have been by the admirers (including Monet, Manet, Sargent, and other painters) who since the 1860s have sought them out in Haarlem.

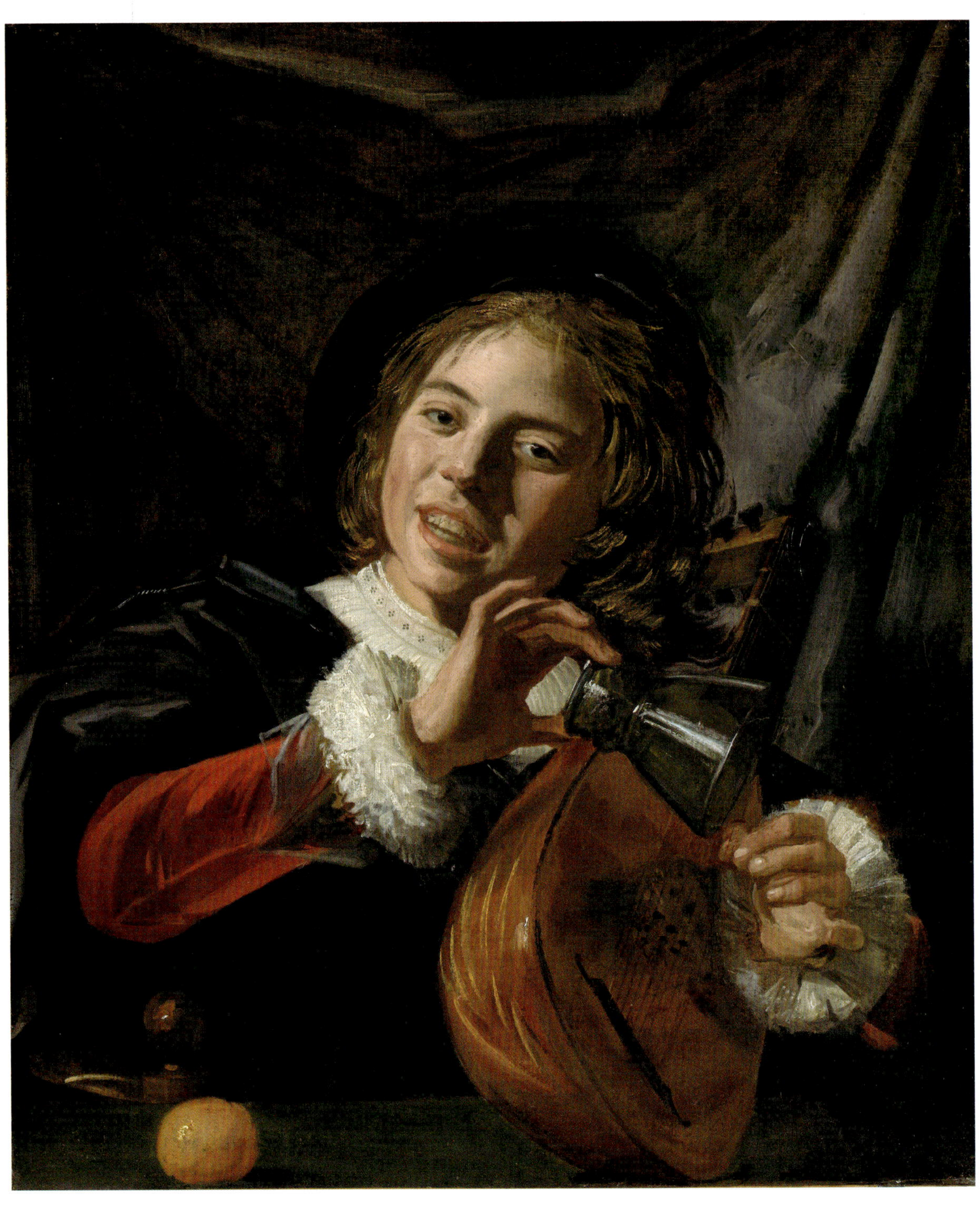

42. Frans Hals. *Boy with a Lute*, ca. 1625. Oil on canvas, 28⅜ x 23¼ in. (72.1 x 59.1 cm). The Metropolitan Museum of Art, Bequest of Benjamin Altman, 1913 (14.40.604). An engraving of a similar composition by the Haarlem printmaker Theodoor Matham (after Gerrit van Honthorst?) refers to the expression "le rubis sur l'ongle" (the ruby on the fingernail), that is, a drop of red wine. Empty glasses were common symbols of mortality, although Hals's carefree musician hardly seems to be looking that far ahead.

acquired by their owners between 1887 and 1909. What really sets the collection apart from those in any other American museum are the four genre scenes, of which the three most important were bought by Benjamin Altman (1840–1913) in 1905 (fig. 18) and 1907 (figs. 14, 42), with his intended bequest to the Museum in mind. The only other significant collection of paintings by Hals in the Western Hemisphere are the eight portraits in the National Gallery of Art, Washington, two of which came from a contemporary of Altman's, Peter Widener (1834–1915), and six from Andrew Mellon (1855–1937), who bought them between 1919 and 1931.[61]

All the early American collectors of Hals placed him in the pantheon of old master painters worthy of possession because of European opinion, mostly in

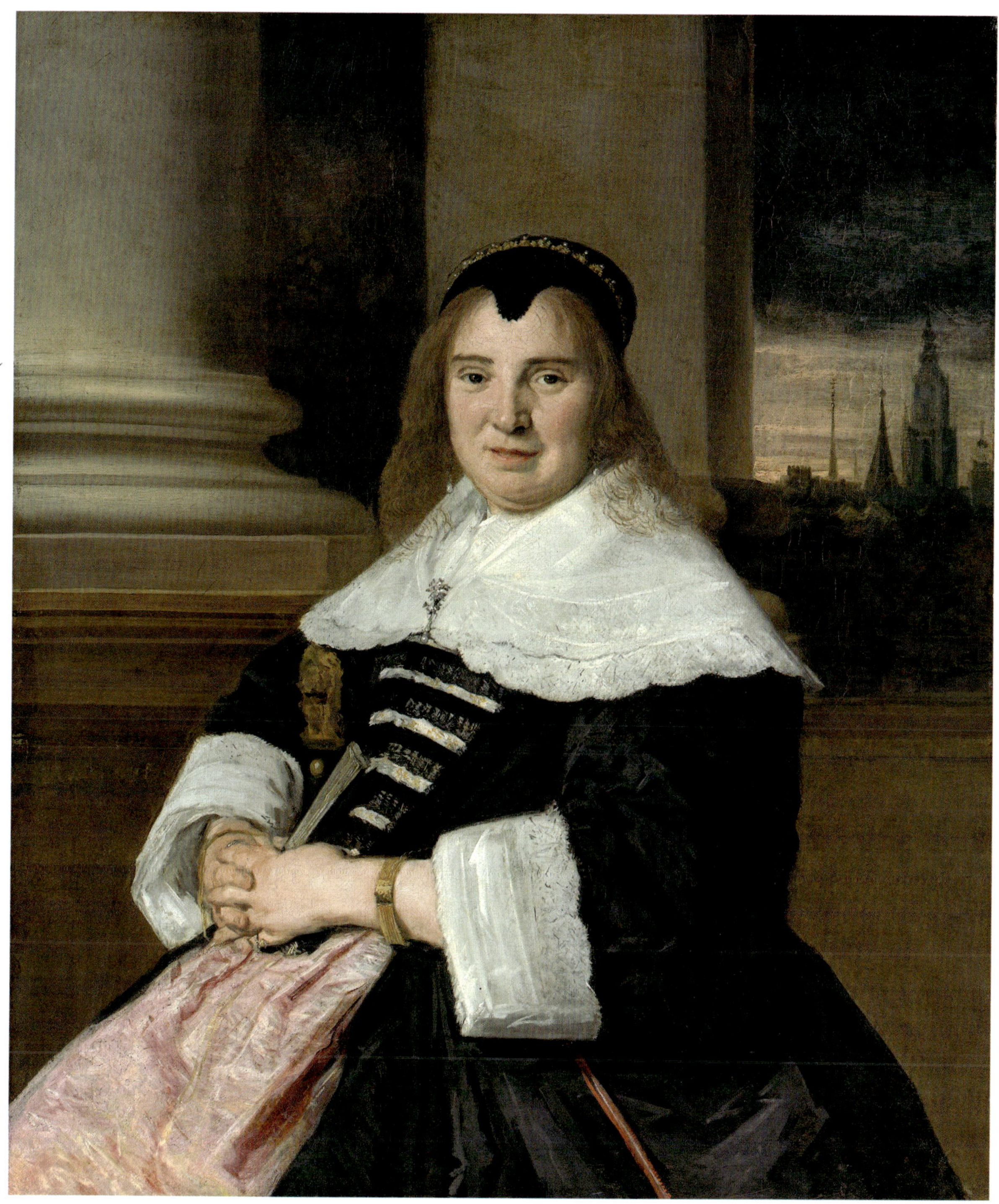

43. Frans Hals. *Portrait of a Woman*, ca. 1650. Oil on canvas, 39⅜ x 32¼ in. (100 x 81.9 cm). The Metropolitan Museum of Art, Marquand Collection, Gift of Henry G. Marquand, 1890 (91.26.10). The background was painted at a later date, probably in the eighteenth century. The picture's likely pendant, *Portrait of a Painter* (Frick Collection, New York), was modernized in the same unsuitable manner.

France. The French critic Théophile Thoré was especially instrumental in the "rediscovery" of Hals in the late nineteenth and early twentieth centuries, and other critics, collectors (such as Lord Hertford, who in 1865 bought *The Laughing Cavalier* [fig. 1] for a spectacular price), and artists helped establish his modern reputation as a painter's painter. As Van Gogh repeatedly insisted, the proper understanding of Hals in the nineteenth century went back to the great Romantic painter Eugène Delacroix (1798–1863), who as a colorist "would have raved . . . , absolutely raved" about the standard bearer in *The Meagre Company*.[62] Thoré championed Hals firstly to support his arguments in favor of modern French painters (as opposed to the academicians) and in the 1860s turned a younger generation's attention to the Dutch master's

44. Édouard Manet (French, Paris 1832–1883 Paris). *George Moore (1852–1933)*, 1873–79. Pastel on canvas, 21¾ x 13⅞ in. (55.2 x 35.2 cm). The Metropolitan Museum of Art, H. O. Havemeyer Collection, Bequest of Mrs. H. O. Havemeyer, 1929 (29.100.55). Moore was an Irish novelist strongly influenced by French writers such as Émile Zola. He studied painting in Paris between 1873 and 1880. The immediacy and broad strokes of Manet's pastel (but not the flattening of the forms) recall Hals's portraits.

45. Frans Hals. *The Fisher Girl*, ca. 1630–32. Oil on canvas, 31¾ x 26¼ in. (80.6 x 66.7 cm). Private collection. With the Ampzing portrait (fig. 40), *The Fisher Girl* is one of the two paintings by Hals lent to the exhibition.

work. The virtues attributed to Hals were virtues not only of style but also of subject and content—including nothing less than the dignity of mankind, political equality, and individual expression. One wonders what Henry Marquand, the railroad financier and Metropolitan Museum president who gave the institution its first three genuine Halses in 1889 and 1890 (figs. 24, 29, 43), would have made of these sentiments. Yet in a broader view, American social ideals, as well as the artistic movements represented by French artists such as Courbet and Manet and writers ranging from Émile Zola to George Moore (see fig. 44), predisposed collectors of the Gilded Age to favor Dutch masters, especially those who treated themes of nature and everyday life.

One can easily imagine how Hals's reputation soared in the age of Impressionism, particularly considering his genre subjects set outdoors, such as *The Fisher Girl* of about 1630–32 (fig. 45).The painting is rarely displayed in public, and it is impossible to appreciate fully from photographs

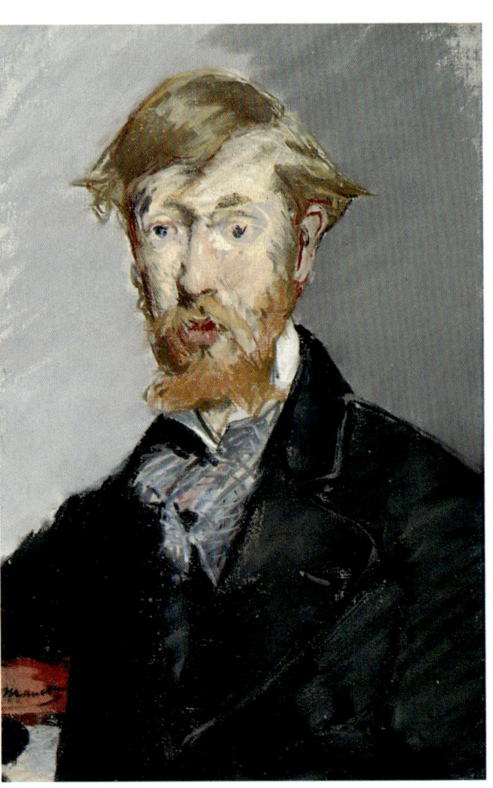

(which tend to flatten the forms) the immediacy of the sensations of movement, light, air, and endless space sweeping behind the figure, up to the clouds and out to sea—not to mention the girl's delight in her silvery treasure (the day's catch has just come in to the beach) and, it would seem, in her encounter with a customer or companion just out of view. Hals painted several pictures of fisher folk in the dunes of the nearby coast, and these popular works were imitated by contemporary followers.[63] This has caused confusion among connoisseurs, a few of whom (including Grimm) toss out the prize catches with the ones that smell fishy. Critical blindness in the face of sheer brilliance is a familiar phenomenon, and in the case of Hals's fisher children and similar figures fails to comprehend how he modified, indeed intensified, his "bold attack" (which Slive describes as "coupled with exquisite pictorial refinement . . . in the *Fisher Girl*") to suit the sun and fresh air and sense of excitement in this type of picture, which unlike formal portraits allowed the artist to push the limits of optical entrancement and technical virtuosity.[64] (A common reaction, for better or worse, to a painting like *The Fisher Girl* is that it is "more Hals than Hals.")

Like several of the Museum's paintings by Hals, *The Fisher Girl* was in Paris during the second half of the nineteenth century and then came directly to New York. It was among the old masters (including works by El Greco and Goya) sold from the estate of the engineer Alphonse Oudry in Paris on April 16–17, 1869, and then was in the extensive collection of European paintings owned by the 2nd Baron de Beurnonville and was sold from his estate in Paris on May 9–16, 1881. De Beurnonville owned ten pictures by or attributed to Hals, but this number must be weighed against his eleven Van Dycks, fifteen Steens, twenty Teniers, and so on. More significant, perhaps, is that *The Fisher Girl* then became one of the

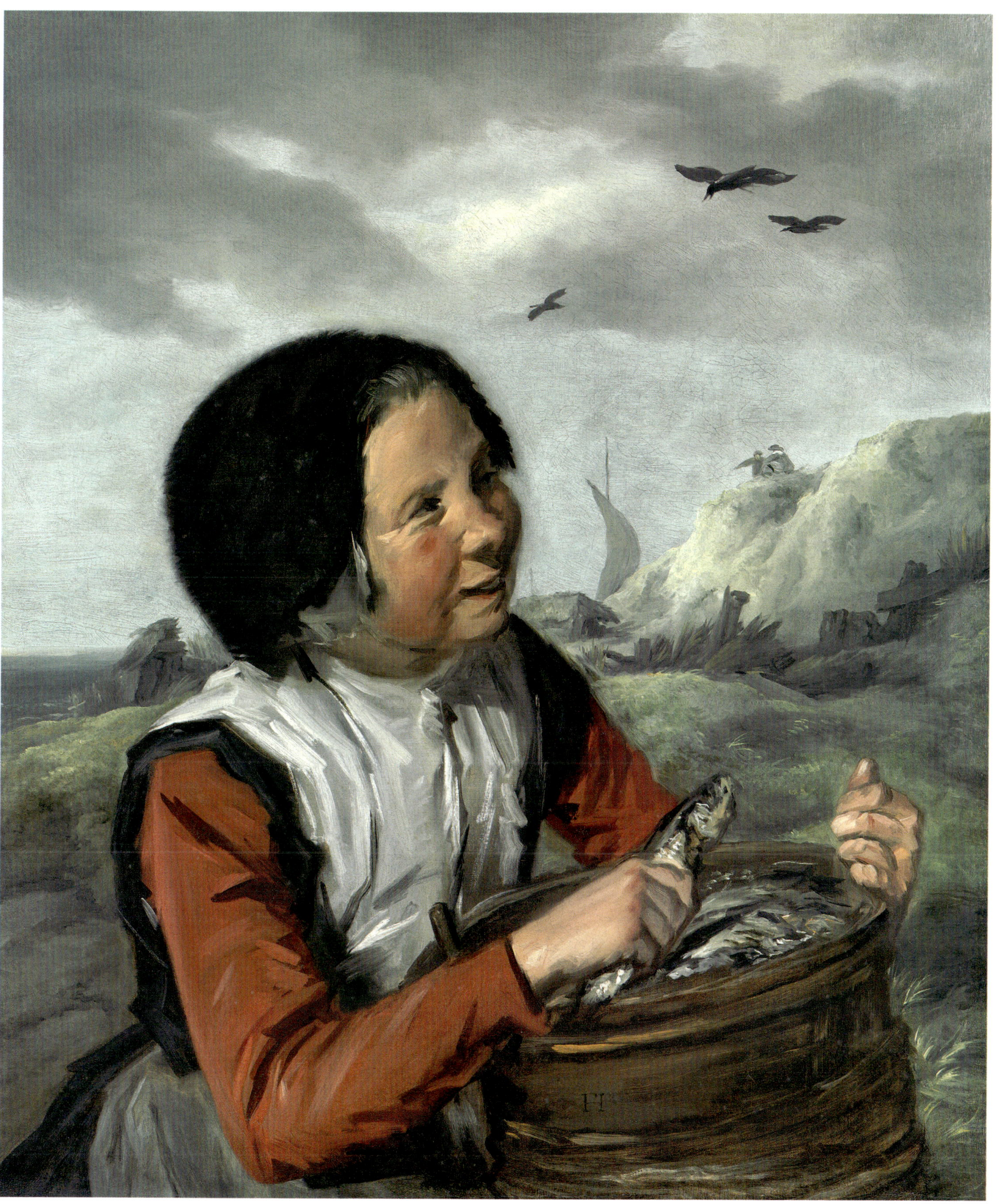

finest of fifty various old master paintings owned by Ernest May (1845–1925), a banker remembered as a major collector of Impressionist pictures and a patron of Degas and Manet. Perhaps to help finance his new country estate, May sold 119 paintings (including the Hals and five Monets, six Pissarros, and four Sisleys), as well as pastels (two by Degas) and drawings, in a Paris auction held on June 2 and 3, 1890. The Hals went to the great dealer of Impressionists and Havemeyer supplier Paul Durand-Ruel, who several weeks later sold it to the New York dealer and collector William Schaus (1821–1892). In Schaus's estate sale on February 28, 1896, the canvas was acquired by Augustus Healy (1850–1921), president of the Brooklyn Institute of Arts and Sciences (now the Brooklyn Museum). The Hals, along with paintings by Monet and Sisley and Healy's own portrait (1907) by his occasional advisor John Singer Sargent, were part of his bequest to the Brooklyn Museum, which sold the Hals in 1967 to the present owner.[65]

In an editorial of September 23, 1883, entitled "Le modernisme de Frans Hals," the forward-looking Belgian art journal *L'art moderne* stressed the importance of Hals's style for the "Franco-American School," consisting of Manet especially but also Sargent, William Merritt Chase, James McNeill Whistler, and others.[66] That "school" included Marquand's advisor J. Alden Weir and the Havemeyers' confidante Mary Cassatt.[67] If for Courbet, Thoré, and other Hals admirers of the 1860s his pictures were significant mainly for their bourgeois subject matter and hearty, vigorous mood, in the 1870s and 1880s the emphasis had shifted to his palette and brushwork.[68] "Frans Hals est un moderne," the Belgian editor claimed, because "his aesthetics, his colors, his composition, his method of working belong to our epoch." This is untrue: Hals was at home in Haarlem during the 1600s. But it is true all the same.

NOTES

1. Joaneath Spicer, "The Renaissance Elbow," in J. Bremmer and H. Roodenburg, eds., *A Cultural History of Gesture: From Antiquity to the Present Day* (Cambridge and Oxford, 1991), pp. 84–128.

2. Gustav Waagen, *Treasures of Art in Great Britain* (London, 1854), vol. 3, p. 36; Houbraken 1718–21, vol. 1, pp. 90–95, translated by Michael Hoyle in Slive et al. 1989, pp. 17–18; Slive 1970–74, vol. 3, p. 64, no. 119.

3. Pieter Biesboer in Slive et al. 1989, p. 23.

4. Slive et al. 1989, p. 14.

5. Houbraken 1718–21, vol. 1, pp. 90–95, translated by Michael Hoyle in Slive et al. 1989, pp. 17–18.

6. Houbraken 1718–21, vol. 3, p. 15; see Michael Hoyle's translation in H. Perry Chapman, Wouter Th. Kloek, and Arthur K. Wheelock Jr., *Jan Steen: Painter and Storyteller* (Washington, D.C., 1996), pp. 93–97.

7. John Ruskin, *Modern Painters*, vol. 1, part 1, sect. 1, and *Praeterita*, vol. 2, chap. 4, in *The Works of John Ruskin*, edited by E. T. Cook and Alexander Wedderburn (London, 1903–12), vol. 3, p. 85; vol. 35, p. 309. Quoted in Ruth Bernard Yeazell, *Art of the Everyday: Dutch Painting and the Realist Novel* (Princeton and Oxford, 2008), p. 24.

8. Quoted in Selina Hastings, *The Secret Lives of Somerset Maugham* (New York, 2010), p. 490.

9. Irene van Thiel-Stroman in Slive et al. 1989, p. 375, doc. 9; Liedtke 2007, pp. 250–51.

10. In Slive et al. 1989, p. 95.

11. Slive 1995, p. 33.

12. Walter Friedlaender, *Caravaggio Studies* (Princeton, 1955), pp. 245, 260.

13. Russ McDonald, *The Bedford Companion to Shakespeare* (Boston and New York, 2001), p. 145.

14. Slive et al. 1989, p. 15.

15. Van Mander (1603–4) 1994–99, vol. 1, p. 294.

16. Slive et al. 1989, p. 133.

17. Slive 1970–74, vol. 1, pp. 48–49, fig. 32 (the drawing); Leeflang and Luijten 2003, nos. 28.2, 98, p. 275.

18. Kolfin 2005, chap. 2.

19. Grimm 1990, pp. 50–51.

20. Van Thiel-Stroman in Slive et al. 1989, pp. 377–78, docs. 17, 22.

21. Liedtke 2007, pp. 262, 988, fig. 282.

22. For the images of 1597 and 1630, see ibid., pp. 260–63, figs. 72, 73.

23. Slive et al. 1989, pp. 162–65.

24. Ibid., p. 378, doc. 22 (November 15, 1616).

25. On Goltzius's responses to the "classicizing manner" of Rubens, see Lawrence Nichols in Leeflang and Luijten 2003, pp. 270–71.

26. Kerry Barrett, "The Artful Hand: Pieter Soutman's Life and Oeuvre." Ph.D. diss., Institute of Fine Arts, New York University, 2009, chap. 2.

27. Peter C. Sutton in Jane Turner, ed., *The Dictionary of Art* (London, 1996), vol. 13, p. 337; Van Thiel 1999, p. 130.

28. Slive (1970–74, vol. 1, chap. 2) discusses "tradition and innovation" in Hals's work between 1610 and 1620 but does not comment on his possible interest in Flemish models. According to Ingeborg Worm (in Turner, *Dictionary of Art*, vol. 14, p. 91), Hals's portraits of that decade "adhere strictly to Dutch conventions established by such artists as Cornelis Ketel and Paulus Moreelse," a claim indicating how little the matter has been studied since Slive's monograph of 1970–74.

29. Atkins 2004, p. 284.

30. Atkins 2006, p. 8. Regarding Hals's "roughly treated passages," Slive (letter to the author, March 25, 2011) would emphasize the painting *Jacob Zaffius* of 1611 in the Frans Hals Museum (Slive et al. 1989, no. 1).

31. On Van Dyck's study heads, see Atkins 2004, p. 286, fig. 4, and Susan J. Barnes et al., *Van Dyck: A Complete Catalogue of the Paintings* (New Haven, 2004), pp. 91–92, nos. 1.94–98.

32. Quoted in connection with Rembrandt's brushwork in Marieke de Winkel, *Fashion and Fancy: Dress and Meaning in Rembrandt's Paintings* (Amsterdam, 2006), p. 126.

33. Liedtke 2007, no. 152, pp. 656, 658n8.

34. Grimm 1990, p. 238.

35. Cornelis de Bie, *Het Gulden Cabinet van de edele vry Schilderconst* (Antwerp, 1661), pp. 281–82, translated in Slive et al. 1989, p. 409. On Vasari, Van Mander, and De Bie, see Atkins 2004, pp. 286–88.

36. Giulio Mancini, *Considerazioni sulla pittura* ([1617–21]; Rome, 1956), vol. 1, pp. 108–9.

37. Translated in Friedlaender, *Caravaggio Studies*, pp. 248–49.

38. Giorgio Vasari, *Le vite de' più eccellenti pittori, scultori e architettori*, ed. Gaetano Milanesi ([1568]; Florence, 1906), vol. 7, p. 452.

39. See, for example, Middelkoop and Van Grevenstein 1990, pp. 88, 93.

40. J. D. Descamps, *La vie des peintres flamands, allemands et hollandaise* (Paris, 1753–63) vol. 1, pp. 360–62; Joshua Reynolds, *Discourses on Art* (1797), edited by Robert R. Wark (New Haven and London, 1975), p. 109, lines 517–25 (Discourse 6, delivered to students of the Royal Academy on December 10, 1774); and J.-B.-P. Le Brun, *Galeries des peintres flamands, hollandaise et allemands* (Paris, 1792–96), vol. 1, p. 71; all quoted (and translated) in Jowell 1989, pp. 62–63.

41. Nikolai Gogol, *Dead Souls* ([1842]; New York, 1997), pp. 20–21.

42. The technical remarks in this and the next two paragraphs are based on the essay by Karin Groen and Ella Hendriks in Slive et al. 1989, pp. 109–27.

43. *Vincent van Gogh: The Letters. The Complete Illustrated and Annotated Edition* (London, 2009), vol. 3, p. 300, letter 536, to Theo van Gogh, on or about October 20, 1885 (not 1886, as sometimes cited).

44. For Courbet's *Malle Babbe* (Hamburger Kunsthalle), see Slive et al. 1989, pp. 236–38, fig. 37a.

45. Houbraken 1718–21, vol. 2, pp. 273–24; see Seymour Slive, *Rembrandt and His Critics* (The Hague, 1953), p. 183.

46. The opportunity to compare local and regional traditions of portraiture was almost completely ignored in Ekkart and Buvelot 2007 (see no. 50 for Van Ravesteyn's civic guard portrait).

47. See Leeflang and Luijten 2003, nos. 15, 51, 55, etc.

48. Slive 1970–74, vol. 1, p. 27.

49. Quoted and translated in Slive et al. 1989, pp. 399–400, doc. 116.

50. Ibid., no. 5 (acquired by the Frans Hals Museum in 2003).

51. On the Havemeyers' Dutch pictures, see Quodbach 2007, pp. 14–17.

52. For the portrait, see Leeflang and Luijten 2003, no. 104.

53. Quoted and translated in Slive et al. 1989, pp. 382–83, doc. 41.

54. See ibid., p. 246.

55. Biesboer in Slive et al. 1989, p. 28; Biesboer et al. 2006, nos. 177, 178, 181 (all in the Frans Hals Museum).

56. Slive et al. 1989, no. 43. The title comes from a Dutch writer of the 1750s who (like a Midwestern tourist among New Yorkers) found all the figures too skinny.

57. Martin Bijl in Slive et al. 1989, pp. 103–8, and see also no. 43.

58. *Van Gogh Letters*, vol. 3, p. 290, letter 534, to Theo van Gogh, October 1885, quoted in Jowell 1989, p. 76.

59. For a list of French artists and the dates they visited Dutch museums, see Chu 1974, p. 6.

60. Slive et al. 1989, nos. 85, 86.

61. Wheelock 1995, pp. 66–91.

62. For this and others of Van Gogh's remarks about Hals and Delacroix, see Jowell's excellent article of 1989, pp. 76–77. For Fantin-Latour's *Homage to Delacroix* of 1864, which in its composition was inspired by one of Hals's group portraits, see ibid., p. 67, fig. 5.

63. See Slive 1970–74, vol. 1, pp. 104–6; vol. 2, pls. 86, 87, 114–19; vol. 3, nos. 55, 56, 71–74; and Slive et al. 1989, nos. 34–36.

64. Slive et al. 1989, p. 228. On p. 230, Slive refers to the fisher girl's left arm as "unfinished," but at a proper viewing distance the change in definition (compare the two arms to the two sides of the face) achieves atmospheric perspective and a fluid transition into the background.

65. On Sargent's responses to and copies after Hals, see Jowell 1989, p. 75, fig. 10. On Healy's role in bringing Impressionist pictures to the Brooklyn Museum, see Sarah Faunce, "Modern French Painting: Collecting in the 1920s," *Apollo* 115 (1982), pp. 276–81.

66. Quoted in Jowell 1989, pp. 74–75.

67. See ibid., pp. 72–73, 75, and Quodbach 2007, pp. 10–11.

68. Chu 1974, p. 112.

SELECT BIBLIOGRAPHY

Atkins, Christopher. "Frans Hals's Virtuoso Brushwork." In *Virtus: Virtuositeit en kunstliefhebbers in de Nederlanden, 1500–1700 / Virtue: Virtuoso, Virtuosity in Netherlandish Art, 1500–1700*, edited by Jan de Jong et al., pp. 281–307. *Nederlands kunsthistorisch jaarboek* 54 (2003). Zwolle, 2004.

———. "The Master's Touch: Frans Hals's Rough Manner." Ph.D. diss., Rutgers University, New Brunswick, N.J., 2006.

Biesboer, Pieter, et al. *Painting in Haarlem, 1500–1850: The Collection of the Frans Hals Museum*. Translated by Jennifer Kilian and Katy Kist. Ghent, 2006.

Chu, Petra ten Doesschate. *French Realism and the Dutch Masters: The Influence of Dutch Seventeenth-Century Painting on the Development of French Painting between 1830–1870*. Utrecht, 1974.

Ekkart, Rudi, and Quentin Buvelot, with contributions by Marieke de Winkel et al. *Dutch Portraits: The Age of Rembrandt and Frans Hals*. Translations by Beverly Jackson. Exh. cat., National Gallery, London, and Royal Picture Gallery, Mauritshuis, The Hague. The Hague and London, 2007.

Grimm, Claus. *Frans Hals: The Complete Work*. Translated by Jürgen Riehle. New York, 1990.

Houbraken, Arnold. *De groote schouburgh der Nederlantsche konstschilders en schilderessen*. 3 vols. Amsterdam, 1718–21.

James, Henry. "The Metropolitan Museum's '1871 Purchase'" (*Atlantic Monthly*, June 1872). Reprinted in *The Painter's Eye: Notes and Essays on the Pictorial Arts by Henry James*, edited by J. L. Sweeney, pp. 52–66. London, 1956.

Jowell, Frances S. "The Rediscovery of Frans Hals." In Slive et al. 1989, pp. 61–86.

Kolfin, Elmer. *The Young Gentry at Play: Northern Netherlandish Scenes of Merry Companies, 1610–1645*. Translated by M. Hoyle. Leiden, 2005.

Leeflang, Huigen, and Ger Luijten, with contributions by Lawrence W. Nichols et al. *Hendrick Goltzius (1558–1617): Drawings, Prints, and Paintings*. Exh. cat., Rijksmuseum, Amsterdam; The Metropolitan Museum of Art, New York; Toledo Museum of Art, 2003–4. Zwolle, 2003.

Liedtke, Walter. "Dutch Paintings in America: The Collectors and Their Ideals." In Ben Broos et al., *Great Dutch Paintings from America*, pp. 14–59. Exh. cat., Mauritshuis, The Hague, and Fine Arts Museums of San Francisco, 1990–91. The Hague, 1990.

———. *Dutch Paintings in The Metropolitan Museum of Art*. 2 vols. New York, 2007.

van Mander, Karel. *The Lives of the Illustrious Netherlandish and German Painters, from the First Edition of the "Schilder-Boeck" (1603–1604)*. Edited by Hessel Miedema; translated by Michael Hoyle, Jacqueline Pennial-Boer, and Charles Ford. 6 vols. Doornspijk, 1994–99.

Middelkoop, Norbert, and Anne van Grevenstein. *Frans Hals: Life, Work, Restoration*. Amsterdam and Haarlem, 1990.

Quodbach, Esmée. "The Age of Rembrandt: Dutch Paintings in The Metropolitan Museum of Art." *MMA Bulletin* 65, no. 1 (summer 2007).

Slive, Seymour. *Frans Hals*. 3 vols. London, 1970–74.

———. *Dutch Painting, 1600–1800*. New Haven and London, 1995.

Slive, Seymour, with contributions by Pieter Biesboer et al. *Frans Hals*. Exh. cat., National Gallery of Art, Washington, D.C., Royal Academy of Arts, London, Frans Hals Museum, Haarlem, 1989–90. London, 1989.

van Thiel, Pieter J. J. *Cornelis Cornelisz van Haarlem, 1562–1638: A Monograph and Catalogue Raisonné*. Translated by Diane L. Webb. Doornspijk, 1999.

Wheelock, Arthur K., Jr. *Dutch Paintings of the Seventeenth Century*. The Collections of the National Gallery of Art Systematic Catalogue. Washington, D.C., 1995.

PHOTOGRAPH CREDITS